THE WAY IT WAS

Old World Italian Recipes For New World Cooks

A.J. Buonpastore

THE WAY IT WAS

Copyright © 2010 by A.J. Buonpastore

All rights reserved. No part of this book may be reproduced or transmitted in any form or by any means without written permission of the author.

Dedication

To my wife Eleanor Nancy Venturella Buonpastore without her love, patience, tasting and testing, editing and proofreading, this book could not have been written.

SMALL TALK

TIDBITS:

Two major ingredients that must always be included in everything you cook.

"COOK EVERYTHING WITH LOVE" AND "LOVE ALL THOSE YOU'RE COOKING FOR".

TIDBITS:

Please be advised, missing in this recipe-cookbook are the use of any measuring devices. They have been omitted intentionally simply because Mom never used them nor did we own any; so they were never used at all, in fact the only thing that I witnessed being used to measure anything was the palm of Mom's hand and occasionally a coffee cup for adding water when she made homemade pasta. The herbs or spices that were used so often were just automatic and the need to measure precisely was not at all necessary. And so for measuring amounts of this or that we will use the size of imaginary coins in the palm of your hand to approximate the amounts needed. Besides we are not scientists in a laboratory and so our measurements are not critical and do not have to be exact, except maybe if we were baking, well then that would be an incorrect statement. Relax and enjoy your time when cooking. When adding salt, pepper, herbs and spices you should by all means taste test as you go. It's really the only way to know for sure whether or not to add or not to add additional salt, pepper, herbs or spices.

THE WAY IT WAS:

In the Buonpastore family we always ate the same thing each week with little variations. Sunday, Tuesday and Thursday were always pasta nights. Monday was soup night, sometime chicken, sometime beef. On Wednesday we ate some type of pasta again only it was mixed with beans {pasta fagioli} or lentils or chickpeas or green peas. On Friday the choice was some type of fish or pasta again cooked with olive oil and anchovies and hot pepper flakes. And if it were not pasta it was some green leafy vegetable like cabbage or dandelions or Swiss chard or escarole with or without cannellini beans, but always with fried garlic in olive oil. Sometimes for dinner it was potatoes in a light tomato gravy with fresh string beans, and sometimes if there was extra money we had a store bought pizza.

On Saturday we ate sandwiches or leftovers if there were any, or Mom made pizza. If you were old enough to be working and supported the household Mom would cook something special. My Mom would cook something special for my brother "Nick", a nice steak with a couple of fried eggs on the side. [I think he bought the steak with his own money]. Nick was our oldest brother who worked very hard, so no one complained. Well, I wasn't old enough to be working but I did enjoy the delicious aroma of the steak and eggs that Mom was cooking. Mom wasn't showing partiality or being mean, that's just the way it was. As a matter of fact I always knew what day of the week it was just by the delicious aromas that emanated from the kitchen.

Remembering that it was the time of the great depression and just having something to eat was a big deal. For that matter it was also a big deal to have something to wear. Conte Luna, Ronzoni and LaRosa were makers of pasta products during those times and they sold their products in cardboard packages just as they do now, thank goodness for that because we used the boxes after they were cut to fit inside our shoes to mend the holes in the soles of our shoes. I wonder if anyone is still doing that? Who said they were the good old days?

TIDBITS:

Knowing and planning your menus ahead of time can save you a lot of time and money when shopping for food.

TIDBITS:

In all of the recipes that follow, for simplicity, we will use the ethnic word "Pasta" for all types of macaroni, noodles, spaghetti etc.

TIDBITS:

Remember when eating was delicious not comfortable. I know I will probably get my cooks hat taken away from me for my criticism of the phrase "comfort food" but I mean no harm, it's my personal opinion and you can go right ahead and continue to use it if it's comfortable for you to do so.

Many TV celebrity cooks often use the phrase "COMFORT FOOD" to describe the foods they cook on their TV shows. Well I have a distaste for the phrase "comfort food". We all know what they mean and are trying to say, I think? But I wish they would stop for a minute and carefully listen to how dumb it really sounds. I think the word comfort was never intended to be used as a descriptive verb associated with food and should be reserved to describe things that we sit on or wear, like chairs. shoes or underwear. So instead of the word comfort I like to use other descriptive words including satisfying, excellent, outstanding, delicious, tangy, sweet, filling. They are in my opinion words that are better suited and much more appropriate to describe the satisfaction and good feeling we get from eating our favorite foods. Think about it; doesn't it sound kind of stupid saying; "Wow that capicola, provolone and hot pepper sandwich I just ate was really comfortable", or the antipasto we ate for dinner was so comfortable. See what I mean? Don't you agree? Come on admit it, you know I am right!!

TIDBITS:

The recipes that follow are easy to make, inexpensive, delicious and satisfying. Most are recipes for dinner. I don't remember having ever eaten cooked meals for lunch, but that does not mean that you can't serve any of them for lunch or any other time you please. They are all special and wonderfully delicious. Please remember they are what they are, recipes. And like all recipes they can be changed to a degree to satisfy your own personal taste. So, if you like to add more or use less of any ingredient by all means do so. It won't change the main concept of the recipe that much.

Some of the recipes that I have chosen for this book may seem somewhat difficult to make but they are not, trust me they are really easy, economical and enjoyed by everyone.

Included are some recipes that most of the time would be missing from our regular dinner table, and for obvious reasons. Mostly because we could not afford to buy the ingredients in them and so they were reserved for the holidays or other special occasions. I am referring to the soup course, the appetizers and the desserts. Soup was generally a dinner by itself and reserved for another day; most certainly always on Monday.

Appetizers weren't always affordable. The appetizers most of the time were a combination of some black and green olives with pieces of provolone cheese or the Gorgonzola (a type of Italian blue cheese) along with fried hot peppers and cut up or sliced pepperoni, or Genoa salami, sometimes anchovies were also set out as appetizers. We were treated to the appetizers whenever there was enough extra money to buy them. Desserts were seldom a part of that day's dinner.

Whenever we did have dessert it may have been fried dough rolled in sugar or sometimes Mom would make pizza. topping it with a little grated red hot pepper and or anchovies.

TIDBITS:

Did you know that there are more than 93 different shapes and names of pasta? No other food satisfies like pasta, especially when you add a delicious meatball or two, a nice salad, fresh crispy sliced Italian bread and a glass of your favorite wine or beverage. For dessert you can have a favorite treat or another glass of wine.

THE WAY IT WAS:

A real treat came when there was a little extra money, money that was hard earned by my father who with a couple of friends played music on Friday or Saturday nights in the local bars and taprooms around the neighborhood. They played all night, free for the saloon keepers and patrons but they were permitted to pass the hat around for tips from the patrons. My father played a great guitar, one of his friends played the violin and the other played a clarinet. They played beautiful music together mostly songs from the old country. Bon Appétit!

Foreword

Keep your table napkin handy because what follows in this recipe-cookbook are the most sought after mouth watering recipes of Italian specialties not found very easily in other cookbooks or anywhere else. Spiced throughout with helpful cooking tidbits for all cooks. Included is an excellent herb chart that takes the mystery and guessing out of what herbs are best used with different types of meats, fish and fowl. The author has also added a sprinkling of his thoughts remembering days that have long gone by; perhaps you can use these thoughts as subjects to spur excellent dinner conversation! Also included are some interesting facts about the author's favorite subject [you guessed it] food.

The recipes in this cookbook are wonderful traditional renditions of some of the foods we ate and enjoyed while growing up in South Philadelphia. They have been used and continue to be used in our family. Most are variations of standard Italian dishes. They are variations because each cook added a little more or less of an ingredient, herb or spice. So you might say that they were all the same but just a little bit different. Many recipes are considered to be traditional and common to most Italian families. They were common in the respect that most ingredients in the recipes were affordable and available year round, some were home grown and preserved. Today many of these old recipes of what was once considered, "peasant food" are today gourmet foods and are very often included on menus in many high-end five star Italian American restaurants.

Table of Contents

Holiday Antipasto Plate 1

Chicken Escarole Soup 3

Fried Italian Sausage 6

Bolognese Gravy 8

Pasta and Tuna Fish 12

Pasta and Clams with Tomato Sauce 17

Pasta and Clams with Olive Oil 19

Pasta and Fried Garlic in Olive Oil 21

Pasta and Fried Anchovies in Olive Oil 22

Pasta and Tuna, Sea Scallops, Capers in Olive Oil 23

Pasta and Tuna, Sea Scallops, Capers with Tomatoes 26

Pasta and Mussels 27

Pasta and Calamari 31

Pasta and Crabs 33

Pasta and Peas 38

Pasta and Cannellini Beans (Pasta Fagioli) 39

Italian Style Roast Beef 42

Italian Style Roast Pork 44

Italian Style Veal Cutlet 48

Italian Style Stuffed and Rolled Beef Braciola 51

Italian Style Stuffed and Rolled Pork Braciola 56

Italian Style Stuffed and Rolled Veal Braciola 57

Italian Style Tomato Gravy 58

Italian Style Meatballs	60
Italian Style Sausage and Peppers	63
Italian Style Veal Parmigiana	65
Italian Style Veal Scaloppini with Peppers, Tomatoes, Mushrooms	67
Italian Style Stuffed Roast Breast of Veal (Bonzette)	71
Italian Style Lamb Stew with Tomatoes, Celery and Peppers	74
Italian Style Chicken Cacciatore (Bianca)	78
Italian Style Chicken Cacciatore with Tomatoes (Russo)	80
Italian Style Chicken Cutlets	81
Italian Style Eggplant Parmigiana	84
Italian Style Zucchini with Tomatoes and Eggs	87
Italian Style Green Beans with Potatoes and Tomato Gravy	90
Italian Style Peas and Artichokes	92
Italian Style Fried Cauliflower	93
Italian Style Celery and Lima Beans with Tomatoes	95
Italian Style Fried Peppers and Eggs	97
Italian Style Fried Potatoes and Eggs	99
Italian Style Fried Tomatoes and Eggs	100
Italian Style Fried Eggs and Grated Romano Cheese	101
Italian Style Fried Eggs, Onions and Mushrooms	102
Italian Style Fried Eggs and Fillets of Anchovies	103
Italian Style Lupini Bean Salad	104
Italian Style Ceci or Chick Pea Salad or Appetizer	105
Italian Style Potato Salad	106
Italian Style Eggplant and Celery with Tomatoes	109

Italian Style Lentil Soup.. 111

Italian Style Holiday Olive Salad or Antipasto.. 113

Italian Style Potatoes Pizziole 115

Italian Style Swiss-Chard and Beans 117

Italian Style Tripe.. 119

Italian Style Calamari with Potatoes and Peas.. 121

Italian Style Stuffed Roasted Peppers 124

Italian Style Hot Chili 126

Italian Style Peppers and Tomatoes 129

Italian Style Steamed Stuffed Artichokes 131

Italian Style Stuffed Clams (Clams Casino) 133

Herb Chart 137

Foods the Burn Calories 138

About the Author 139

Photographs 140

Holiday Antipasto Plate

Holiday Antipasto Plate

(Jemma's Favorite)

Ingredients:

Chunks of sharp provolone cheese, or chunks of mozzarella or any cheese that you prefer, there are so many you can choose

1 can of medium sized pitted California ripe black olives drained

1 jar of green Spanish style pimiento stuffed olives or a jar of Sicilian green olives

1 can of rolled caper stuffed anchovies

1 stick of Italian pepperoni sliced thin or cut into chunks if you prefer

1 jar of roasted red peppers sliced into small pieces

1 jar of hot vinegar peppers [Pepperoncini]

1 can of Italian style tuna in olive oil

1 can or jar or a frozen package of artichoke hearts

1 can of chick-peas drained and rinsed under cold water

Plating:

Using your decorating skills place the above ingredients in piles on the leaves of romaine lettuce, using the leaves to make little pockets. Sprinkle or drizzle olive oil over everything. That's all there is to it, simple wasn't it. Serve with bread sticks or crackers or thin sliced crusty Italian bread. Of course you can substitute add or remove any of the ingredients above.

TIDBITS:

Escarole soup seems to be everyone's favorite and can be made in a variety of ways. The following may seem a bit much but it is not, it's very easy. The hardest part really is the cleaning of the escarole.

Chicken Escarole Soup

CHICKEN ESCAROLE SOUP

Ingredients:

You will need, depending on the size of the escarole, about two large heads of escarole washed under cold water, drained, torn into smaller or bite size pieces

1 large whole fresh chicken breast cut into bite size pieces

1 large can of chicken broth

Salt and pepper to taste

2 large carrot sticks-chop one into 1 inch pieces. Dice 1 carrot set it aside

4 stalks of celery with leaves - cut three stalks into 1 inch pieces - chop the leaves into small pieces - Dice 1 stalk celery and set it aside

1 medium size onion cut into quarters

¼ bunch of fresh parsley chopped into small pieces or dried leaf parsley

Garlic powder

TIDBITS:

To thoroughly clean escarole, cut off the head or tip of the core of escarole about an inch or so from the tip allowing the leaves to separate. Plug up your sink to allow your sink to full at least halfway. Run the cold water over the leaves shaking and dunking them into the cold water. Drain the water and repeat as many times as needed to get the leaves clean. Wash escarole leaves to remove any sand or earthly debris, discard any leaves that may be brown or otherwise discolored. Cut or tear into small bite size pieces, place the cleaned leaves into a colander and set aside.

Cooking chicken escarole soup:

In a large soup pot add 2 quarts of water

Set heat to medium; add salt about a quarter size

Bring to a boil

Add chicken breast

Add in the large pieces chopped carrot

Add in the large pieces and the leaves of the celery

Add in the quartered onion

Add in ½ of the chopped parsley save the other half

Shake in a small amount of garlic powder

Add in a very small amount of black pepper, the pepper can be omitted completely if desired. Bring to a second boil.

When the vegetables are soft and the chicken is thoroughly cooked remove from heat and strain all to another pot. Discard the vegetables. Chop the chicken into bite size pieces if you have not done so already and set aside.

Add the large can of chicken broth to the strained broth you just made.

Add in the cleaned escarole leaves.

Add the rest of the ingredients, that is, the remainder of the carrots, celery, parsley, do not add the chicken just yet.

Bring the heat to medium low and let the escarole cook until tender.

Taste and add salt if needed. When the escarole leaves become tender add the chicken, allow the chicken a few minutes to get warm, then serve.

As I stated at the start of the soup recipe, there are variations. You can add tiny meatballs. Use the same recipe for making meatballs found elsewhere in this book, just make them tiny or smaller.

You can add white rice if you like.

You can add a small can of tomato sauce.

You can add Acini Pepe (tiny bebe sized pasta).

You can add Orzo if you like.

You can make it with meatballs and chicken if you like.

You can serve the soup with your favorite cheese, Romano or Parmesan.

You can make it with or without the chicken or the meatballs.

This recipe is very versatile and you can customize it any way you like.

(Nikki's Favorite)

For working mothers whose time is limited use one 46 oz can of chicken broth, add in one 8 oz can of tomato sauce, heat to a boil. In a separate pot, cook one pound of any small pasta according to directions on box. When cooked, strain pasta and add to soup. Cook together for about a minute, then serve. The kids will love it!

Fried Italian Sausage

FRIED ITALIAN SAUSAGE HOT OR SWEET:

(Sal's Favorite)

Ingredients:

2 or 3 lbs. Italian Hot or Sweet Sausage

Olive oil

Onions - optional

Hot or Sweet Peppers - optional

Red Wine - optional

From the supermarket or butcher shop buy enough hot or sweet Italian sausage. Figure at least two pieces per person. In a large frying pan place a little cooking oil, I prefer to use olive oil but it's not necessary, corn oil or any vegetable oil will do.

For a little extra flavor you can add a little red wine, an ounce or two would be just fine. Be careful when you add the wine, it sometimes has the tendency to flare up. Fry the sausages until they are well done remembering to pierce them with a sharp pointed knife while they are cooking to release some of the fatty juices that are in the sausages. Be sure to turn them often to keep them from burning. After they are cooked set them aside and serve them with a salad. Where's my napkin, my mouth is watering again.

THE WAY IT WAS:

Do you remember when guys used to shoot [craps] or play dice games in the street, and kids pitched pennies? When the cops came to break up the game everyone ran like heck leaving money and everything behind in the street.

THE WAY IT WAS:

Do you remember pegged leg pants and zoot suits?

TIDBITS:

Next is a recipe that you will love to make because it's so simple. I could almost guarantee that it will become one of your favorites. It's called Bolognese. I am not sure how to spell it but I do know how to make it. It is a variation of the tomato gravy that we made above with the addition of ground meat in it.

A lot of people make a big fuss over this recipe thinking it is difficult to make because it is so scrumptious. But in reality it is quite simple. In fact the real truth is, it's harder to spell the name than it is to make.

THE WAY IT WAS:

Do you remember when soft pretzels cost a penny each? I sold them when I was a kid to make a few bucks. I bought them at the bakery at two for a penny and sold them at a penny each. I had a little basket with a clean cloth to lay the pretzels on and a jar of mustard. Hey, I made enough to go to the movies and maybe buy some candy.

Bolognese Gravy

BOLOGNESE GRAVY:

Ingredients:

4 - 28 oz cans of Italian crushed tomatoes

Garlic powder

Dried oregano flakes

Dried sweet basil leaves - Use fresh basil leaves if available

Dried Italian flat leaf parsley, any dried parsley flakes will do

Use fresh parsley if available

Salt and pepper

Hot red pepper flakes are optional

1- 1/2 pounds of mixed ground beef, pork and veal

Olive oil

Cooking Bolognese gravy:

In a large gravy pot add enough olive oil to just cover the bottom of the pot.

Using medium heat allow the oil to get hot enough to sauté the ground beef, pork and veal.

Add the meat to the hot oil.

Stir as often as necessary and adjust the heat to keep the meat from burning.

Add salt and crushed black pepper to taste.

Add the 4 cans of Italian crushed tomatoes.

Bring to a slow boil then lower the heat setting to simmer.

Add in all of the remaining herbs and spices.

Garlic powder amount, use the size of a nickel in the palm of your hand

Dried oregano amount, use about the same as the garlic powder

Dried sweet basil leaves amount same as above

If fresh sweet basil, use about a dozen leaves chopped

Dried Italian flat leaf parsley, use the same as the sweet basil

Add the hot red pepper flakes if desired to taste

Let the gravy simmer for at least 1 hour

Serve over your choice of pasta

Serve with fresh sliced crispy Italian bread

TIDBITS:

There are many variations of tomato gravy that you can cook using the same herbs and spices. What will change the flavor is the addition of the different meat or fish items that you add. So far we have tried meatballs, sausage, braciolas. Other additional gravy recipes can be found elsewhere in this cookbook.

TIDBITS:

The previous tomato gravies were made with a variation of meat items. Meatballs, sausages and braciola and other meat items make a wonderful pasta gravy individually, however you can mix the different meat items and combine as many of each as you like. Often on special occasions or holidays the three types of meat were combined.

The meat items that we used in the previous recipes are traditional. But by no means are you limited to just using those three. Any meat item can be used, the only prerequisite I suggest is that you sauté or lightly fry it before adding it to the tomato gravy. And then continue to cook it until it is thoroughly cooked in the gravy.

THE WAY IT WAS:

Many of you won't believe this but I remember when sneakers cost just $2.00 (Keds) a pair; today they call them tennis shoes, walking shoes, running shoes, etc. We all pay through the nose for the designer's name. When you think about it they should pay us to wear them, after all we are advertising their name. Oh well, that's just the way it is.

THE WAY IT WAS:

Do you remember when city workers picked up trash using horse drawn wagons? In the cities most homes were heated by burning coal, the end result of the burned coal were ashes. The ashes then were taken from the heaters and placed into baskets or containers of some kind and put out onto the curbside to be picked up and taken to a city dump.

TIDBITS:

Meat items are not the only ingredients that can be used to make a wonderful tasting pasta gravy. The following recipe is made with canned tuna {not a type-o}. I did mean canned tuna. Of course you can use fresh tuna when it is affordable and available.

Pasta and Tuna Fish

PASTA AND TUNA FISH:

Ingredients:

2 - 6 oz. cans of white solid tuna fish packed in water

2 28oz cans of Italian style crushed tomatoes

One half of one medium sized bell pepper red or green

Salt to taste. Use very little because the canned tuna may have salt in it

Hot Red pepper flakes - optional

Crushed black pepper to taste

Garlic powder

Sweet basil

Oregano

Making the Gravy:

Start with enough olive oil to thinly cover the bottom of a six quart pot.

Over medium heat add one half of one medium size red or green bell pepper chopped into small ½ inch pieces.

Add just a little salt and crushed black pepper to taste.

Sauté the pepper for 10 to 15 minutes or until the pepper becomes soft stirring occasionally to keep it from burning.

After the pepper has cooked sufficiently, add the two cans of well drained tuna into the pot with the bell pepper, stir to incorporate the tuna with the bell pepper and olive oil. Stir carefully to keep the tuna from falling apart completely.

The previous procedure usually takes about five minutes or less depending on the heat of the pot. Now it is time to remove just the tuna and bell pepper mixture from the pot, and set aside. Leave the olive oil in the pot.

Add four cans of Italian style crushed tomatoes to the pot.

Set heat to medium. While stirring bring the tomatoes to a light boil.

Add in garlic powder about the size of a dime.

Add in the sweet basil if the dry leaves are used about the size of a nickel will do. If fresh leaves are used, cut eight leaves more or less into small pieces. I don't think you can ever use too much fresh sweet basil.

Add the dry oregano about the size of a nickel. Oregano is very strong in flavor and would dominate the taste of whatever it is that you may be cooking, so be a little careful when you do use this herb.

Let the tomatoes and herbs simmer for at least thirty minutes or more.

When you are satisfied that the gravy has cooked long enough add the tuna and pepper back into the pot. Let the tuna cook another five minutes, not much longer because if you do the tuna will dissolve completely, that's not really bad but I love my tuna in chunks.

Serve the tuna with gravy over a bed of Angel Hair pasta, or Linguini, or any favorite pasta.

THE WAY IT WAS:

Hey! Do you remember knickers? They were a sort of short pants worn about knee-high, they were gathered with elastic like sweat pants are today. The pair I had were brown corduroy that made a swishing sound with each step I took. I never hated anything as much as I hated wearing those knickers. Other boys thought you were a sissy for wearing them and they would tease the heck out of you. They were worn with long knee-high argyle style socks. It was demanded that I wear them to school. Maybe that's what started my hatred for school at an early age. There's probably a Freudian lesson to be learned here, that being, don't force your children to wear clothing they are not comfortable wearing. As in my case there were underlying reasons that I just did not want to tell Mom about. I have an old photograph of me wearing those pants; I love to throw darts at it.

TIDBITS:

Let's have a sip of our favorite beverage and get back to cooking. To help you decide on what type of wine would be best served with your seafood and pasta meals consider any of these three: Sauterne, Rhine wine, or Chablis. Remember though any beverage is good if it is the beverage you like best. My rule for what wine to drink with certain foods is very simple. If it tastes good to you then that is the wine you should drink, period.

Pasta and Clams with Tomato Sauce

PASTA AND CLAMS:

Pasta and Clams with Tomato Sauce the Red Sauce:

This seafood gravy can be made with or without tomatoes. They are equally delicious and very easy to make. They are often referred to as clams in red or white sauce. Lets start with the recipe for clams in red sauce.

Ingredients:

1 half of one medium size finely chopped green or red bell pepper

1 small can of whole baby clams

2 small cans chopped clams in water or clam juice

1 28 oz. can of crushed Italian style plum tomatoes

1 small bottle of clam juice

1 large can of chicken broth. Vegetable or beef broth can be substituted.

Fresh or dried Italian flat leaf parsley; about the size of quarter if you are using dried leaves. If fresh parsley is used chop about the size of a quarter.

Fresh or dried sweet basil leaves. Use the same amount as parsley.

Dry red hot pepper flakes. Use only if you like your gravy a little tangy.

Salt, use very little and only if you really need it. Most of the other ingredients in this recipe have salt added.

Crushed black pepper, use about the size of dime. 8 cloves of finely chopped or sliced garlic. Garlic powder may substitute for fresh cloves.

Olive oil.

Making Clams with Tomato Gravy:

In a large heavy pot, over medium heat put in enough olive oil to thinly cover the bottom of the pot. When the olive oil is hot add in the finely chopped fresh garlic stir constantly until the garlic is a golden brown color.

Remove the garlic from the pot and set aside. If you are going to use garlic powder instead of the garlic cloves, do not add the garlic powder to the hot oil by itself it will burn quickly, just add it to the chopped bell pepper and let it sauté for a few minutes until the peppers get tender.

When you are satisfied the peppers have softened, add in the can of baby clams and the two cans of chopped clams; you can at this time also return the garlic to the pot.

Lower the heat to a simmer. Add in the bottle of clam juice and the chicken broth. Add in the can of crushed tomatoes, stirring often as needed to keep from burning. Add the parsley and sweet basil. Add salt if needed. Add the crushed red pepper flakes and the black pepper.

Let simmer on low heat for at least forty-five minutes. Serve over a bed of Linguini or you favorite pasta; with sliced crispy Italian bread.

Pasta and Clams with Olive Oil

PASTA AND CLAMS WHITE WITH OLIVE OIL:

Making the White Clam Sauce:

The major and perhaps the only difference between the red and the white clam sauce is you do not use tomatoes in the white sauce. You can if you desire to use capers. Capers are the buds of the acacia plant. They are usually packed in 2 or 3 oz jars with water and vinegar and salt, most of the time they are very salty, rinsing them in cold water before using is a good idea.

You can also add ripe black olives to this very versatile seafood dish. Just sauté the capers or the black olives or both when you add the clams and let them simmer together.

THE WAY IT WAS:

Mom made this recipe very often on Friday because money was very tight in those days and most of the time by Friday Mom was broke and could not afford to buy enough fish for everyone so, to at least have something to eat she made aglio e olio. Which simply is pasta topped with fried garlic or anchovies in olive oil. Crushed red hot pepper flakes were also used sometimes. It was delicious.

Pasta and Fried Garlic in Olive Oil

PASTA AND FRIED GARLIC IN OLIVE OIL [Aglio e olio]:

This easy economical recipe is so easy to make you will be amazed how wonderful it really tastes because it was made in so short a time, and to add to that it costs next to nothing to buy the ingredients. You probably have all of the ingredients just sitting in your pantry or refrigerator right now.

Ingredients:

Fresh cloves of garlic depending on the size of the garlic cloves 6 or 8 will do, sliced very thin or use garlic powder to taste

Olive oil

Crushed red pepper flakes

Salt

Spaghetti or Linguini or any of your favorite pasta

Making Aglio e Olio:

In a large heated frying pan add enough olive oil to cover the pan then add just a little more; remember that the olive oil will be your sauce in this recipe. When the olive oil is hot, add in the thinly sliced garlic cloves and let them brown; WARNING: thin garlic slices will fry quickly, do not let them burn. If fresh garlic is not available, use garlic powder about the size of nickel. Quickly add the red pepper flakes; pepper flakes will also burn quickly so be careful not to let that happen - stir rapidly-salt to taste. Add the salted pasta water to the olive oil if the pasta is too dry. Doing this will not effect the taste. Serve over a bed of Linguini or your favorite pasta.

PASTA AND FRIED ANCHOVIES IN OLIVE OIL:

Pasta Aglio e Olio and Aligi:

For a different taste to the olive oil and garlic mixture and one that I like very much is the simple addition of canned anchovies in olive oil. Anchovies come packed a few different ways, canned or in jars, with or without capers rolled or flat. Try them, you will love them, I am sure. Add them to the hot oil for a few minutes or until they melt or have almost completely dissolved after which you add the garlic and other ingredients as above.

Anchovies are notoriously salty; when using them you will not need to salt whatever you're cooking any further.

When boiling the water for the pasta you generally add in salt to flavor the pasta, be careful not to add too much salt. Use half as much salt in the water if you are going to use anchovies. Also try to remove any of the fine anchovy bones. Sometimes they are not filleted as well as they should be.

TIDBITS:

Try the following recipes, especially if you like seafood and pasta, they are really very delicious.

Pasta and Tuna, Sea Scallops, Capers in Olive Oil

PASTA AND TUNA, SEA SCALLOPS, CAPERS IN OLIVE OIL:

(Marina's Favorite)

Ingredients:

1 can of anchovies with capers in olive oil

2 cans of solid white tuna fish in water

1 pound of sea scallops

1 14 oz. can chicken broth or stock

Olive oil to thinly coat the bottom of a large pan

One six ounce can of tomato paste [optional]

4 dried hot chili peppers [optional]

Garlic powder

Dried parsley or fresh Italian flat leaf parsley

Dried oregano

Grated Parmesan or Romano cheese [optional]

Salt and ground black pepper

1 pound of Spaghetti or Angel Hair or any of your favorite pasta

Cooking and Preparing:

In a large pasta cooking pot prepare enough water to cook the angel hair estimating about a ¼ pound of pasta per person - Bring the water to a rolling boil, adding just a little salt.

Do not add the pasta to the pot just yet. Angel Hair or any thin pasta takes only a few minutes to cook.

In a large frying pan over medium heat add olive oil to thinly cover the pan.

Add 1 can of anchovies with capers to the olive oil stirring continuously until the anchovies have all disintegrated leaving just the capers.

Drain the water from the two cans of tuna then add the tuna to the pan with the capers. Add in the sea scallops. Be sure the scallops are completely thawed if using frozen ones. Stirring frequently for about 5 minutes or until the scallops have absorbed some of the olive oil and liquid from the pan.

Remove the tuna and scallops from the pan and set aside.

Add a bit more olive oil if needed to lightly cover the bottom of the pan.

Add in one can of chicken broth or stock.

Add in 4 dried hot chili peppers [optional].

Add in the garlic powder about the size of a dime.

Add in about 6 sprigs of fresh finely chopped parsley or dried leaf about the size of a dime.

Add in the dried oregano about the size of a dime.

Sprinkle in a small amount of salt and ground black pepper.

Bring to a slow boil over medium heat. Now add back into the pot the tuna and scallops. Remove from heat and set aside.

Using the pot of boiling water you prepared above add your favorite pasta. When the Angel Hair or your favorite pasta has cooked to your liking [do not overcook] remove from the pot and drain. After they have sufficiently drained add them to the tuna and scallops, stir and serve with fresh sliced Italian bread and a green salad.

THE WAY IT WAS:

Do you remember the fruit and vegetable venders? We called them hucksters, selling fruits and vegetables door to door? In fact I did some selling of fruits and vegetables myself. Sometimes they came through the city's back alleys behind the houses calling out loudly the items they were selling. "Heyyyy get your "pepperrrs" get your tomatoes here".

Pasta and Tuna, Sea Scallops, Capers with Tomatoes

PASTA and TUNA, SEA SCALLOPS, CAPERS with TOMATOES

Pasta and Tuna, Sea Scallops, Capers with Tomatoes:

This delicious recipe is exactly the same as the recipe above or elsewhere in this recipe book (Pasta and Tuna, Sea Scallops, Capers in Olive Oil), except for the addition of one 6 oz. can of tomato paste.

Add the tomato paste to the hot olive oil and anchovies stirring until the paste is absorbed into the oil. Then continue with the remainder of the recipe as presented.

Pasta and Mussels

PASTA AND MUSSELS IN TOMATO GRAVY:

Ingredients:

2 pounds of fresh mussels

1 pound of your favorite pasta, make it Spaghetti

3 stalks of fresh celery, chop 1 stalk into tiny pieces as small as you can chop it, cut the other 2 stalks into 1 inch pieces

1 red sweet bell pepper diced

1 green bell pepper diced

1 long hot Italian green pepper diced [dry crushed red hot pepper can substitute for fresh] but is optional

2 - 28 oz. cans of crushed tomatoes

2 cloves fresh garlic crushed or sliced thinly or chopped in very tiny pieces [substitute garlic powder if preferred]

Olive oil

Salt and pepper

Oregano

Fresh sweet basil

TIDBITS:

Most mussels bought today at supermarkets are farm raised and require very little cleaning. However, you should rinse them off under cold water and remove any beards or debris and discard any open mussels before cooking. I discard any mussels with a broken shell. If you are not sure about it, discard it. It's best to be safe than sorry.

Cooking Pasta and Mussels:

Over medium heat

Lightly cover the bottom of a large sauce pot with olive oil

Add in and lightly brown the fresh garlic cloves or garlic powder

Add in the fresh celery

Add in all of the peppers

Sauté until celery and peppers are tender and have absorbed some of the olive oil

Stir in the canned crushed tomatoes

Add in about the size of a quarter in the palm of your hand the oregano

Add in the same amount of dried basil or eight to ten leaves of fresh basil

Add salt and pepper to taste-bring to a boil

Lower heat and simmer for at least ½ hour

After tomato sauce has cooked for at least a ½ hour

Add in the fresh cleaned mussels

The mussel shell starts to open when they are cooked; give them a chance to open up but do not let them overcook.

Try to synchronize the cooking of the mussels with the cooking of the pasta

In a large pasta pot bring to a boil enough water to cook the one pound of pasta - add salt to taste

Drain the pasta when they are cooked to your liking. Place them in a large serving plate, ladle the mussels and gravy over the pasta and serve with crisp Italian bread and a green salad.

THE WAY IT WAS:

Talking about mussels and seashells always reminds me of course of the beach. Do you remember getting suntanned without worrying about getting skin cancer? We often laid on the beach for hours, not giving any thought to sunburn. At night we all suffered and used jars of Noxzema to help with the pain.

Pasta and Calamari

PASTA AND CALAMARI:

Ingredients:

2 pounds of calamari cleaned, with arms or tentacles removed, cut into ½ inch rings, include the arms and or tentacles if you desire

Rinse and drain the calamari

2 - 28 oz. cans of crushed Italian style plum tomatoes

Garlic powder about the size of a nickel or 2 cloves of fresh garlic chopped into very fine pieces

Salt and pepper

Hot red crushed pepper - optional

Olive oil

Fresh parsley sprigs if available or dried leaf about the size of a nickel

Dried oregano about the size of a dime

Cooking the Calamari:

In a large pot add enough olive oil to thinly cover the bottom of the pot, let the oil get very hot. Add the drained calamari to the olive oil, be careful of the hot oil splashing when adding the calamari. Stir quickly and thoroughly. Add in salt and pepper to taste. Cook for a couple of minutes or until tender but do not overcook or the calamari will get chewy. Remove calamari from pot and set aside.

Add to the same pot the 2 cans of tomatoes and bring to a slow boil, stirring to keep from burning and sticking. After the tomatoes have come to a slow boil, lower heat to simmer and then stir in all of the above ingredients except the calamari. Let simmer for at least

45 to 60 minutes. When you are satisfied the tomatoes are cooked to your liking (always taste test) add the calamari. Let the calamari soak in the tomato gravy for a minute or two then remove from the heat and ladle over a plate of any of your favorite pasta. Enjoy!!

Pasta and Crabs

PASTA AND CRABS:

You just gotta have Spaghetti! Well not really, you can use any long thin pasta you desire. I like Spaghetti as it has a little more body to it than say Angel Hair or some of the others.

THE WAY IT WAS:

It reminds me of the days when our kids were growing up; they just loved crabs and Spaghetti. I remember one warm summer afternoon I had made a large pot of the crab gravy. We all ate outside on our picnic table. The kids ate the crabs and Spaghetti as though it was going to be their last meal.

They were so full of gravy; it was everywhere, all over their faces, in their hair and up to their elbows. Napkins were just useless so we decided to turn the garden hose on to clean them up. They just loved it. It was one of those precious times that you just never forget.

TIDBITS:

Crabs make wonderful tasting gravy. I don't know of anyone who does not like the sweetness of the crabmeat. It has become a real treat in our family.

I do not make it as often as I should, only because trying to find the large crabs became a hassle for me. Also, the price of large crabs are getting much too expensive. Crab gravy is so easy to make.

Ingredients:

Large fresh crabs, the amount of crabs you use depends upon the number of people you will serve. If you are only interested in making the gravy then the crabs could very well be small and the amount of crabs that you use really does not make much difference.

I have used both large and small crabs and as few as six. And as far as I can tell there is no great difference. I have often used packages of frozen crabs, when the fresh crabs are out of season; they are okay for flavoring the gravy and will do in a pinch, but I prefer fresh live crabs. For our recipe we will use six live large fresh crabs.

The crabs must be cleaned before you cook them.

In order to control the crab's attitude, just place them in your refrigerator for a little while. The coldness makes them docile and easier to handle.

If you prefer not to clean them yourself have the person you bought them from clean them for you, just be sure that they are fresh.

2 - 28oz cans of crushed Italian tomatoes

2 - 28oz cans of tomato sauce

6 cloves of fresh garlic; you may substitute garlic powder if fresh is not available or if you just prefer the ease of garlic powder

Fresh sweet basil; you may substitute dried leaves

Dried oregano leaves

Fresh Italian flat leaf parsley

One half of one medium size red sweet bell pepper

Olive oil

Salt and crushed black pepper

Making Crab Gravy:

In a large gravy pot over medium heat add enough olive oil to barely cover the bottom of the pot. Remove the backs and clean the crabs. If you purchased crabs already cleaned just rinse them off under cold water to be sure all the debris is gone.

Place the cleaned crabs in the hot olive oil.

Be careful of splashing the hot oil with the wet crabs.

Sprinkle all of the dried herbs and spices onto the crabs.

Turn the crabs so that they are seasoned on both sides.

When the crabs turn somewhat orange in color, remove them from the pot.

The crabs usually cook in just a few minutes. You do not want to overcook them. After you remove the crabs from the pot add in the canned tomatoes.

Add in more of the sweet basil - Salt and pepper to taste.

Using medium heat, bring the tomatoes to a boil, lower the heat and let the tomatoes simmer for at least thirty minutes. When the tomatoes are cooked to your satisfaction add the crabs to the pot and stir for a few minutes.

Serve on a bed of your favorite pasta. Make mine Spaghetti!

THE WAY IT WAS:

When we had visitors, aunts and uncles or just friends they were always treated to whatever was available to eat and drink; they sat and talked about the old country. Most of the time they spoke Italian and sometimes in broken English. They always sipped homemade wine; the wine was made by a proud family friend, (who was also the neighborhood shoemaker), occasionally given to my father for his valued opinion. That usually happened when a new barrel of wine was opened.

As a kid I was not allowed to drink the wine but I was allowed to taste it. And when I got a little older I was asked sometimes by my father to go to the shoemaker or shoe repair shop and buy a bottle of wine. The shoemaker always made very good wine. It was stored in barrels down in his cellar. Selling wine was a little thing he had going for him on the side. In those days everyone had a little thing going on the side to make a few extra dollars.

Pasta and Peas

PASTA AND PEAS:

This recipe is so very easy to make and everybody likes it.

Ingredients:

1 can of sweet green peas drained, or 1 pound bag of frozen green peas

1 16oz box of elbow pasta or any short cut pasta will do

½ of a medium sized onion

Olive oil for sautéing the peas

Salt and pepper to taste

Crushed red pepper flakes (optional)

Cooking the Pasta and Peas:

In a large pot, bring enough water to boil to cook the 1 pound box of elbows.

Bring water to a rolling boil, add the elbows.

While you're waiting for the elbows to cook, in a large frying pan, over medium heat add enough olive oil to sauté the peas and the onions. Sauté the onions first. When the onions are done add the can of sweet peas.

Lower heat to simmer, cook for 5 minutes. Add salt and pepper.

Add the optional hot crushed red pepper.

When you are satisfied that the elbows are cooked, drain the elbows in a colander. Place the drained elbows in a serving bowl. Pour the peas and onion mixture onto the elbows. Mix lightly and serve.

Pasta and Cannellini Beans (Pasta Fagioli)

PASTA AND CANNELLINI BEANS [PASTA FAGIOLI]:

"You don't have to be Italian to love this recipe"

(Margie's Favorite)

Ingredients:

1 - 19 oz. can of cannellini or kidney beans

1 - lb. of Ditalini or any elbow type pasta

1 - 28 oz. can of tomato sauce

Olive oil

2 stalks of celery with leaves washed and sliced into very thin slices

1/2 of a red or green bell pepper, core and pith removed chopped finely

Salt and pepper to taste

3 or 4 garlic cloves optional, garlic powder may be substituted. The cloves of garlic can be cut in half or even smaller pieces will do, we are just going to flavor the olive oil with the garlic. And if you have decided to use the garlic powder, enough should be used to sprinkle the top of the beans while they are sautéing.

1 green long hot pepper optional chopped into ¼ inch or very small pieces

Oregano dried leaf about the size of a dime in the palm of your hand.

Parsley fresh flat leaf if available about 3 or 4 sprigs chopped if not dried leaf will do.

Sweet basil fresh about 6 leaves if available, if not use the dried about the size of nickel in the palm of your hand.

Cooking the Pasta and Beans:

In a large soup pot add enough olive oil to coat the bottom of the pot. Over medium heat:

Add in the optional garlic pieces.

Add in the celery and the peppers.

Sauté the garlic, celery and the peppers until they are tender.

If you feel that the garlic pieces are getting too brown, remove and discard them; they have done their job and you will not need them any longer.

When you are satisfied with the consistency of the celery and the peppers, add in the can of cannellini beans. Add in salt and pepper to taste.

Add in a sprinkle of garlic powder. Add in the can of tomato sauce.

Add in the sweet basil - Cover the pot and lower the heat to simmer - Cook for about 30 minutes.

TIDBITS:

By now you probably know that one of my favorite foods is pasta. Pasta is a staple in most Italian homes. Or it used to be. It really should be a staple food item for everyone not only Italians. It is very versatile and it is nutritious and good tasting. There are probably a hundred different ways to cook pasta and each of them would make a satisfying and delicious meal.

Italian Style Roast Beef

ITALIAN STYLE ROAST BEEF:

TIDBITS:

I laugh to myself each time I am in my local deli and see the shelf sign under the roast beef, "Italian roast beef"; what does that mean? What makes it Italian? Did an Italian chef make it? Was the roast made in Italy? Was the steer born in Italy? Or was it made simply using Italian herbs and spices. I think the latter is probably the right answer.

THE WAY IT WAS:

When I was growing up I seldom had the pleasure of eating roast beef, Italian or otherwise. We were lucky enough to have a meatball once in awhile and or a piece of a braciola. In fact the only time I remember eating roast beef was when I was old enough to hang out with the boys and old enough to go to the neighborhood bar and restaurant, to play darts, have a beer and eat a roast beef sandwich. The name of this fine Italian eatery is called Bomb-Bomb and I wonder where it got it's name??? Rumor has it that it was the target of a disagreement, however, this South Philadelphia restaurant and bar is still at the same location and the food is still excellent!! (Stop in and check it out)! The beef at the bar was great and the beer was only 10 cents a glass, cold and delicious. Tap beer and only 10 cents a glass, could you imagine that? Incidentally, my friend Frankie and his beloved wife Reggie, the owners of this fine establishment were responsible for introducing me to my beautiful and wonderful wife back in 1955 and for that gift I owe them a world of gratitude and my heartfelt thanks.

TIDBITS:

To conclude I would say that if you wanted to make your next roast beef Italian style. just add the following herbs, basil, oregano and bay leaves, a sprinkle of garlic powder, salt and pepper and a small amount of olive oil. This is how I suggest you use the herbs and spices to roast the beef. Regardless of the cut of meat you are going to use drizzle a small amount of olive oil on the meat- rub in the oil on all sides of the meat. Sprinkle or shake on the basil, oregano, garlic powder, salt and pepper and rub the herbs and spices into the meat covering all sides. Leave two or three bay leaves whole. If possible refrigerate the beef for a couple of hours, until you are ready to roast it, overnight would be great but not necessary. What you are really doing is marinating the beef in the oil and herbs. When ready, place the roast in the roasting pan fat side up and let it roast at 325 degrees. When you are ready to serve, just say out loud that you are serving "Italian roast beef".

TIDBITS:

Do not use high temperatures when you roast beef or any other meat for that matter, it causes the meat to toughen and shrink. Roast your meats at low temperatures, 325 degrees would be the average temperature. Always keep the fatty side up in the roasting pan. Score the fat of the roast every couple of inches. When testing with a fork try not to pierce the meat, it lets the juices run out. Use a meat thermometer for best results.

Italian Style Roast Pork

ITALIAN STYLE ROAST PORK TENDERLOIN:

Roast pork, try the following recipe, you will love it and so will everyone that is lucky enough to share it with you.

Ingredients:

Whole pork loin; about 8-10 pounds

Olive oil

Garlic powder

Salt and Pepper

Rosemary

Oregano

Parsley

Cracked or ground black pepper

1-16 oz can of beef broth, you could use chicken or vegetable broth as a substitute

1 jar of hot cherry peppers in vinegar

6 bay leaves

Roasting Pork Tenderloin:

Preheat oven to 400 degrees.

Place the pork loin in a large roasting pan. If the loin is very large cut the pork loin in half for easier handling. Drizzle olive oil over the entire pork loin, rub in the oil and garlic powder.

Place the pork loin in the preheated oven, uncovered and fat side up. Let the pork loin brown slightly.

Remove the roast from the oven and add all of the dry herbs, salt and pepper; be sure to spread the herbs evenly but not heavy.

Pour the can of chicken or beef broth around the roast.

Add or place the bay leaves around the roast.

Add 8-10 hot cherry peppers around the roast to taste.

Pour about 2 tbsp of the vinegar from the jar of the hot cherry peppers.

Reduce the oven temp to 325 degrees.

Cover the roast and place it into the oven and let it slow cook until the meat is tender or falls apart easily when pierced with a fork.

Check it from time to time as the roast may take up to several hours to completely cook depending on the size of the roast.

TIDBITS:

When you remove the roast from the oven you can serve it a couple of ways. If you want to make sandwiches you could start to pull the roast apart while it is still hot; it seems to be easier when the meat is hot. Try adding provolone cheese to your sandwiches for a great extra treat. Or you can let it cool a little and slice it and serve it with your favorite vegetables. A great accompaniment would be broccoli rabe or hot Italian potato salad.

THE WAY IT WAS:

Do you remember when going to the movies just cost a dime? When I was growing up it was really something special to go to a movie. And look at what we got for just a dime. The movie house that I went to most often was called the Colonial. It was just a block away from my home. On Saturday the movie show started with a real live local talent show. Kids would compete for weeks and the winner would get the big prize that was a new bicycle, I can't remember how long the competition went on for but I am sure it was for weeks. It was fun to see and hear some of the local talent who auditioned. But it was also humiliating for those who had no talent because the crowded movie patrons booed and really showed no mercy when they heckled them relentlessly.

After all they wanted to the see the cartoons and the feature movie. They felt that those who had no talent were just wasting time; I felt sorry for some of them especially the ones who could not sing at all, but they had a lot of guts.

After the local talent show the lights dimmed and the movies started. They showed some cartoons and after the cartoons they showed the world news, then some type of short. After that they showed the coming of attractions. When the coming of attractions were over they showed the continuation of last weeks chapter. It could have been the Green Hornet or the Lone Ranger or Buck Rogers or anyone of the many feature chapters that were going on at that time.

After that they would show some small short comedy maybe the Three Stooges or the Keystone Cops. Then possibly the house lights would go on before the main feature to allow you to go to the refreshment stand to buy candy or go to the restroom. After a few minutes the house lights would dim and they started to show one of two features. They always had double features on Saturday.

Lots of people often brought their lunch with them in a brown paper bag. You could sometimes spend a good six, seven or more hours at the movie and all that for only ten cents.

Some movie houses gave away sets of dinner plates or carnival glass bowls or other free items, these were given away one piece at a time to attract steady patrons who would come back week after week to try to make complete sets of dinner plates. Sometimes when people weren't careful the dishes fell off their laps and broke and everyone, for reasons that are still a mystery to me would applaud. And that's just the way it was. They were the good old days. Let's get back to cooking.

TIDBITS:

I think if I had to choose a variety of meat I liked best of all I would have to choose veal. When cooked properly it is very tender and mild tasting.

Italian Style Veal Cutlet

ITALIAN STYLE VEAL CUTLETS:

Ingredients:

Thin sliced veal cutlet from the butcher, plan on at least a ¼ pound per person.

Flour optional see the note on using flour below.

Breadcrumbs if you are using the plain unflavored, you will need to use the dry herbs listed below. If you use flavored Italian style breadcrumbs do not add any other of the dried herbs listed below.

Eggs

Salt and Pepper

Grated Locatelli Romano cheese

Dried leaf oregano

Dried leaf parsley

Garlic powder

Olive oil

TIDBITS:

You can eliminate using flour if you prefer and just use the egg mixture and breadcrumbs.

Preparing and Frying Italian Veal Cutlets:

In a large frying pan add in enough olive oil to completely cover the bottom of the pan. Set the heat to medium. Get the olive oil hot.

Using a plate or a baking pan place enough plain unflavored breadcrumbs into it to coat the amount of cutlets that you are going to fry.

If you are using plain breadcrumbs then add the dried herbs to flavor the breadcrumbs, use about the size of a quarter of each herb for each pound of cutlet. Add as much as the size of a silver dollar of the Locatelli Romano cheese for each pound of cutlet to the herb mixture or more if desired.

For exceptional great taste finely chopped fresh Italian flat leaf parsley should be used in place of the dried parsley.

Add salt and pepper to the dry mix.

The Locatelli Romano cheese in itself is somewhat salty keep that in mind when you add the salt and pepper to the dry mixture of herbs.

Add a small amount of garlic powder the size of a dime for each pound of cutlet to the dry mixture.

Beat two eggs with a little bit of milk or cold water in a mixing bowl.

Dredge the slices of cutlet through the flour, coating both sides if flour is used. Then, dredge the flour-coated cutlet through the egg mixture coating both sides. Then, dredge or press the cutlet down into the dry breadcrumb mixture coating both sides.

Place the breadcrumb-coated cutlet into the pan of hot olive oil carefully to avoid splashing of the hot oil. Do not overcrowd the frying pan. Fry the cutlet on one side until it is a golden brown then turn and fry the other side. The cooking time will vary depending on thickness of the cutlets. Serve with a green leafy salad.

Italian Style Stuffed and Rolled Beef Braciola

ITALIAN STYLE STUFFED AND ROLLED BEEF BRACIOLA:

TIDBITS:

This recipe seems to be a favorite of everyone. Usually made along with other meats like meatballs and sausages as part of the gravy for pasta, it can be used as a stand-alone for dinner.

The main ingredient of course is the beef. If the cut of meat used is tough and not tender then all your effort will be wasted. I have used several different cuts of beef including thin sliced sandwich steaks. I found what works best is the same cut of meat Mom always used and that is the top of the round cut about 3/16" to a 1/4" thick and approximately 4" wide and 8" or 9" and even 10" long. Keep in mind that these measurements are approximate and only used as a guide. You're not building a house so the sizes aren't that critical.

When I was a kid I worked in a butcher shop and the butcher had this machine he used to tenderize different cuts of meat. I don't have a tenderizing machine in my kitchen and I doubt it if very many people do. But I do have a heavy all metal hammer like tool with pointed nubs on either side that I use to pound the cuts of meat. The pounding breaks down nerves and tenderizes the meat. Whenever I feel there is a need to tenderize a cut of meat I pound the heck out it. You can also use the flat side of a cleaver or other type of kitchen tool you may have at your disposal if you think there is a need to tenderize a cut of meat before cooking it.

Without further comment let's get on with making a delicious braciola.

(Anthony's Favorite)

Ingredients:

Top of the round beef slices approx. 3/16"-1/4" thick x 4" x 8" or 9" long

Grated Locatelli Romano cheese

Salt and pepper

Garlic powder or finely chopped cloves of garlic

Fresh chopped parsley, dried parsley flakes will do if fresh is not available

Grated red pepper flakes - optional

California golden raisins - optional

Fresh chopped sweet basil leaves

Prosciutto, sliced or cut into small chunks - optional

Grated Parmesan cheese can be substituted for Locatelli Romano

The use of any herb or spice is a matter of personal taste and preference, as is with garlic. I have used it in every way possible including rubbing the cloves over the meat; I have smashed and crushed and cut it thin enough to see through. But garlic powder works best for me most of the time. One word of caution here, don't use garlic salt. It's hard to tell how much salt or garlic is in the mixture.

Preparing the Braciola:

At your work area place long strips of wax or foil paper on the tabletop, this will make cleaning a little easier when you are through. Before you touch the meat you should set up a little mass production area. If you are going to use toothpicks place them nearby, you will need three or four per slice of meat. If you are going to tie the braciolas, place a ball of butcher string and a scissor near your work area. Place as many slices of meat on the aluminum foil paper as you can fit without crowding. Place all of the herbs and spices nearby. You will need to use salt and pepper as well.

With all of the ingredients at one side of the work surface start adding the filling moving from left to right or right to left doesn't matter it's just a way to know that you don't forget to include one ingredient or the other.

This procedure is great if you're making a bunch of braciolas but if you are only making one then it's not that important. Cover the entire cut of meat with all of your ingredients. It doesn't matter which ingredient goes on first or last, but I do it like this:

First sprinkle salt and black ground pepper on all the pieces

Then add the garlic powder or if using the garlic rub, do that now

Add the Locatelli cheese or the Parmesan cheese

Add the parsley

Add the sweet basil

Add the optional golden raisins

Add the optional prosciutto

Add the optional red pepper flakes

Sun dried raisins can be used. If used, just a few on each slice of meat is all that is needed. The combination of hot pepper and sweet raisins is sooooo delicious.

Starting at the smallest end part of the meat, roll up the stuffed meat. Roll each piece and tie with butcher string, make as many turns with the string as necessary to keep it together.

Prepare a large skillet or frying pan, coat the pan with olive oil and heat to medium.

Place each of the stuffed braciolas with the seam end down into the hot oil. Place as many as the pan can hold without crowding. When each braciola is browned sufficiently, remove from the frying pan and place them into your tomato gravy that should have been cooking while you were creating these delicious braciolas.

Allow them to cook in the gravy for at least an hour.

Enjoy the braciolas with a nice tossed green salad.

TIDBITS:

Beef braciolas are no doubt my favorite way to eat beef, but coming very close to it is another favorite; that is making braciolas with pork cutlets. Try it and see for yourself you will love them.

The problem that I have is I can't find pork cutlets that are as large as the top of the round beef slices, but other than that they are getting to be very popular in my family and requested more and more often. If you are using pork slices, you will want to use some Rosemary, using about the size of a dime in the palm of your hand spread the dried Rosemary leaves over the meat slices. Rosemary is really great with pork; you can use it on veal and beef if you like or it could be omitted.

Beef, pork and veal braciola take a little more time and effort but they are worth it. However, I must warn you, once you start with the braciola they will become everyone's favorite. You may want to save making them just for holidays or special occasions. The recipe for braciola can be the same regardless of the type of meat that you select. The meat slices should be at least four inches wide and about ten inches long. They could vary in thickness but not more than a quarter inch thick. My family prefers thin sliced meat; the choice is yours. Top of the round cuts are usually best.

Depending on how many you will be serving, figure at least two braciolas per person but take into consideration the size of the meat slices and whether you will be serving any other meat items along with the braciolas.

TIDBITS:

I remember when my Mom first put the raisins in the braciola, I thought it was going to spoil the whole dinner and my father was going to be mad at her for doing so. Well as it turns out I was wrong.

The first time that you make braciolas might seem a little daunting or difficult and time consuming but after they are eaten I am sure you will agree that it was worth any and all of the trouble.

While we are on the subject of making braciolas let me add that the recipe given here may be a standard in my family but by no means is it absolute or are you limited to the fillings that are in my recipe. You are only limited by your own imagination.

Other fillings could be Italian ham or prosciutto de Parma, pine nuts, different cheeses, different herbs and spices, the list can go on and on. Try sautéing very finely chopped red bell pepper and a little bit of the Italian long green hot peppers and using them for a braciola filler. Hmmm.

Italian Style Stuffed and Rolled Pork Braciola

ITALIAN STYLE PORK BRACIOLAS:

If you want to try pork braciolas, just duplicate everything in the recipe that I have written for beef braciolas.

Italian Style Stuffed and Rolled Veal Braciola

ITALIAN STYLE VEAL BRACIOLAS:

And of course you can also do it with veal cutlets as well for another winner. Just duplicate everything in the recipe that I have written for beef braciola.

Italian Style Tomato Gravy

ITALIAN STYLE TOMATO GRAVY:

Ingredients:

4 - 28 oz. cans of crushed tomatoes

Salt and a little crushed black pepper to taste.

Sweet fresh chopped basil leaves, use about a dozen leaves if not use the dry herb about the size of a quarter in the palm of your hand.

Oregano, use about the size of a dime.

Parsley, Italian flat leaf preferred, if the fresh leaf is available chop and use about the size of a half dollar, if not use the dry herb about the size of a quarter.

Garlic powder, use about the size of a quarter in the palm of your hand.

All measurements are approximate-add more or less to satisfy your own personal preferences.

Making the Gravy:

Using a large heavy bottom pot mix in all of the above ingredients starting with the tomatoes then followed with the herbs and spices. Over medium heat bring to a boil stirring as often as needed careful not to burn the tomatoes.

After it starts to boil lower the heat to its lowest setting and simmer. The gravy recipe above is outstanding and delicious. It could be used as is without the addition of any meat items or other ingredients. Now that we have started the gravy cooking let's make the meatballs.

Italian Style Meatballs

ITALIAN STYLE MEATBALLS:

I'm not one to brag but I must take a bow when it comes to making great tasting meatballs. Follow this recipe as close as you can and you will get a standing ovation, I guarantee it.

(Brianna's Favorite)

Ingredients:

From any supermarket or butcher shop buy 1 1/2 pounds of mixed ground pork, veal and beef. Generally the three are packaged together and weigh about 1 1/2 pounds. This recipe is for 3 pounds of ground meat.

In a large bowl mix all of the meat with the following ingredients:

3 large eggs or 4 medium eggs

2 handfuls of unflavored breadcrumbs (about 4 oz.)

Salt and black pepper about the size of a dime

Fresh Italian flat leaf parsley chopped about the size of a half dollar

Grated Locatelli Romano cheese about 6 oz.

Add a dime size amount of garlic powder

Add a dime size amount of oregano

Add a dime size amount of sweet basil leaves

California Golden Seedless Raisins (optional)

Mix all of the ingredients well, then form into golf ball size shapes.

Frying the Meatballs:

In a large frying pan or heavy cast iron skillet place enough olive oil in the pan to fry the meatballs. When using olive oil to fry keep in mind that olive oil will burn or smoke if the heat setting is too high. So if you prefer you can use corn oil or other vegetable oil. When the oil is hot enough you can start frying the meatballs.

Let the meatballs fry to a light brown or gray color, at this point using a spoon with holes so the oil will drip back into the frying pan, we are going to take the meatballs out of the frying pan and place them into the simmering tomato gravy. Continue to do this until all of the meatballs are fried. (As I write my mouth is watering)! Don't forget to stir the gravy occasionally; we don't want it to burn. Let the meatball gravy simmer for at least two hours.

TIDBITS:

Some do and some don't like raisins in their meatballs. The only way you will know for sure if you like your meatballs with them is to try it once on a few of them then next time you make meatballs you will know whether or not to use them. Raisins tend to make the meat taste sweet.

If you enjoy meatballs that are soft and moist (and who doesn't?) - go easy on the breadcrumbs, just add a couple of slices of white bread with all the edges removed and moistened with tap water to each pound of ground meat. Pull the bread apart into very tiny pieces and mix it thoroughly with the meat and all of the other ingredients.

I find that using two packages of about one and a half pounds each makes approximately forty meatballs the size of golf balls. I think that's a good size for a couple of reasons. The most important reason is that when you are cooking pork it should always be thoroughly cooked and never ever be undercooked. The other reason is that being of a somewhat smaller size they absorb more gravy and thereby make the meatballs more flavorful and juicy.

Cook in the tomato gravy for at least one hour. If you want you can serve and eat the meatballs just fried without tomato gravy. If you intend to use them just fried then they must be fried for a longer period of time to be sure that they are thoroughly cooked on the inside. Just lower the heat and fry for a longer time until the inside of the meatball is grey in color. Serve with a nice leafy green salad or make delicious meatball sandwiches with fried hot peppers on an Italian roll.

The gravy as stated above with a little variation can be used a couple of times at least during the week or anytime you choose. (Be sure to wrap securely and refrigerate or freeze all leftovers). Use the leftover gravy that we made above to make another delicious dinner.

Consider using different pastas; remember there are at least 93 shapes and types to choose from. Spaghetti, Perciatelli, these are long straw shaped, Shells (large or small), Ziti, Penne, Rigatoni, and for a real treat you may want to choose Ravioli, or potato Gnocchi, Cavatelli, etc.; the list is endless. Then you can choose or select other meat items. Some choices could be: fried pork chops, beef braciolas, Italian sausage, chicken, pork braciola or veal braciola.

Italian Style Sausage and Peppers

ITALIAN STYLE SAUSAGE AND PEPPERS:

Ingredients:

Hot or sweet Italian sausage use one or the other or combine each type.

Depending upon how many people you intend to serve allow a minimum of at least 1/4 pound per person. Understand also the sausages have a natural tendency to shrink a little when they are thoroughly cooked so allow a little extra for that.

Let's assume you will be cooking about 3 pounds of sausage.

(1 1/2) pounds of hot sausage cut into 2" pieces

(1 1/2) pounds of sweet sausage cut into 2" pieces

2 - large green bell peppers washed, cored and sliced into 1/2" strips, pat dry with a kitchen cloth

2 - large red bell peppers washed, cored and sliced into 1/2" strips, pat dry with a kitchen cloth

1 - small Vidalia onion - optional, cut or sliced into 1/4" pieces

Olive oil to coat the bottom of a large frying pan

Salt and pepper

Oregano

Garlic powder

Preparing:

In a large frying pan lightly coat the bottom with olive oil

Heat the olive oil on medium setting - don't let it get too hot

Add in the peppers - Add in the salt and pepper - Add in the garlic powder

Add in just a light sprinkle of oregano

Fry the peppers until they start to caramelize a little

Add the optional Vidalia onion. At this time let onion cook until it becomes soft. When the peppers and onions are cooked remove them from the pan and set aside. Add more olive oil at this point, if needed, to fry the sausage. Add the sausage to the pan and fry until completely cooked. You will know that the sausage is cooked when the edge of the sausage gets a crispy edge and a dark brown color. In the process of cooking and just before you believe the sausages are fully cooked poke the center of the sausages with a sharp pointed knife; doing this releases some juices that are in the sausage some of which is unneeded fat. In a clean frying pan, or if you like, use the one you have been using, just wipe it clean with paper towels. Now combine the peppers and the sausages in a pan and cook together for another ten minutes.

Italian Style Veal Parmigiana

ITALIAN STYLE VEAL PARMIGIANA:

Ingredients:

Veal Cutlets (Breaded and Fried)

Tomato Gravy

Sliced or grated mozzarella cheese

Preparing:

This is so easy!

Using some leftover tomato gravy and veal cutlet recipes found elsewhere in this cookbook, prepare a baking pan {sprayed with nonstick oil}. Place a single layer of fried veal cutlet; spoon on to the top of the veal cutlet some tomato gravy - use enough gravy to just cover the cutlets.

Add the sliced or grated mozzarella cheese to the top of the cutlets with the gravy. Now place the pan into a 350 degree preheated oven until the cheese is melted and bubbly. Serve with a side of Spaghetti and a leafy green salad. Mamma Mia it's so delicious!

THE WAY IT WAS:

Do you remember the Burma shave verse signs along the sides of the highways? The signs were placed at intervals for maybe a quarter mile, I think there may have been six signs to a verse with a few words on each sign, the following is just one of many, "ITS BEST FOR ONE WHO HITS THE BOTTLE TO LET ANOTHER USE THE THROTTLE".

Italian Style Veal Scaloppini with Peppers, Tomatoes, Mushrooms

ITALIAN STYLE VEAL SCALOPPINI WITH PEPPERS, TOMATOES AND MUSHROOMS:

TIDBITS:

This recipe is a real treat for everyone and can be made with sweet red and green bell peppers and/ or long hot Italian peppers or a combination of both.

In our recipe below we will use a combination of red and green bell peppers and the long hot Italian peppers. It can also be made very economically by using packaged precut veal pieces, or if your budget can afford it you can use the veal cutlet cut into smaller pieces.

Keep in mind though if you do use the precut pieces they are not as tender as the veal cutlet and will need to be cooked a little longer.

The difference in cost between the two is very significant, the veal cutlet generally runs about $14.00 - $16.00 a pound while the precut pieces average about $4.00 - $6.00 a pound. If you want you can consider veal chops but you will have to trim the chops and cut them into small pieces.

Ingredients:

2 - pounds of veal either precut pieces or cutlet

1 - pound of white mushrooms; cut into ¼ inch slices

1 - pound of red bell peppers cut into ½ inch strips

1 - pound of green bell peppers cut into ½ inch strips

1 - pound of long hot Italian peppers {optional}

1 - 28 oz can of tomato sauce

1 - 28 oz can of crushed tomatoes

Garlic powder

Salt and pepper

Dried oregano

Fresh sweet basil - use the dried if the fresh is not available

Italian flat leaf parsley

Olive oil

Preparing:

In a large heavy bottom pot or Dutch oven use just enough olive oil to lightly cover the bottom of the pot - using medium heat.

If needed trim any gristle or fat from the precut veal pieces then add to the hot oil. If you are using cutlets, cut them into 2 inch pieces before adding them to the hot oil.

Add salt and pepper to taste.

Do not over fry the veal just let them quickly turn gray a little then remove the veal from the pot and set aside. Add the sliced mushrooms to the pot adding more olive oil if needed. Fry the mushroom slices until they start to brown or get a little crispy.

Add a sprinkle of garlic powder to the mushrooms.

Add all of the peppers to the cooked mushrooms.

Add the can of tomato sauce.

Add the can of crushed tomatoes.

Add in the fresh sweet basil, use 6 leaves chopped into small pieces, otherwise use about the size of a dime of the dried.

Add in the dried oregano about the size of a dime in the palm of your hand.

Add in the fresh flat leaf Italian parsley use at least 6 sprigs chopped finely, if dried use about the size of a dime.

Add a little salt if desired. Return the veal to the pot - lower the heat to a simmer and let everything cook until the veal pieces are tender. Stir occasionally - taste for needed salt and tenderness of the veal. Veal scaloppini makes a wonderful sandwich. Make the sandwiches with crispy Italian rolls from the bakery or serve with a side dish of white rice and a crispy green leaf salad.

THE WAY IT WAS:

When we were kids in our early teens crashing weddings was kind of a regular thing for us to do on a Saturday or Sunday night. It gave us something to do, a place where we could meet girls and dance. But best of all it was where we could eat free.

Although most of the time the menu was limited to sandwiches and potato salad, soda and beer, a far cry from what is offered in today's lavish weddings. The sandwiches were mostly ham or cheese, although I was told that some well-to-do families had roast beef sandwiches. I never saw them. The sandwiches were handed out over the bar where the soda and draught beer was being served. There was strict control over who got what kind of sandwich and someone related to the bride or groom generally handled control.

If the server didn't know who you were you got the cheese sandwiches and only people that were known to that server were given the ham sandwiches. Often that idea did not sit well with some people and arguments and problems started between the bride and groom's families. It really didn't matter to us whether it was ham or cheese it was something to eat. The live band [there was always a live band] played all the favorite songs of the time and it was great fun to watch the old timers dance. I often think how nice it really was back then in the good old days. It just seems that everyone was satisfied with everything they had no matter how little it was.

TIDBITS:

I better get back to my recipes, I kind of get carried away when I start to think and talk about the good old days. Try the next veal recipe. There isn't much meat on this cut of roast but the stuffing makes it all worthwhile.

Italian Style Stuffed Roast Breast of Veal (Bonzette)

ITALIAN STYLE STUFFED ROAST BREAST OF VEAL: (BONZETTE)

Ingredients:

A one pound roast will serve at least 2 people

This roast is mostly for people who love the tasty cheese, egg, and breadcrumb stuffing. There isn't much meat on this cut of veal but what meat there is, is wonderful.

The breast of veal generally comes with a pocket ready for stuffing from your butcher. If by chance it doesn't, just ask and I am sure your butcher will be glad to accommodate you.

2 or 3 eggs depending on the size of the cut

Milk or cold water to thin the eggs

1/4 to 1/2 - pound of grated Locatelli Romano cheese

1/2 - pound of plain breadcrumbs

1/2 - of one small onion finely chopped

1/2 - of stalk of celery finely chopped

Salt and pepper

Garlic powder

Crushed hot red pepper flakes about the size of a dime

Dried oregano the size of a nickel

Fresh Italian flat leaf parsley 12 sprigs finely chopped, if dried use about a quarter size

Olive oil

Plump sun dried raisins (optional) about 18-24 raisins

Several large toothpicks

Cooking Breast of Veal:

Preheat oven 325 degrees

Sprinkle a little olive oil over the entire roast - rub olive oil into the roast with a little salt, pepper, and garlic powder.

In a mixing bowl add all of the remaining ingredients.

Mix with hand or fork but do not over mix. The mix should not be on the dry side and not too wet or loose.

Stuff the mixed ingredients into the pre-cut pocket, secure and close the pocket with the toothpicks.

Place the roast in the pan and let it cook until the roast is browned and roasted tender to your liking. The time it takes will depend of course on how large the roast is.

THE WAY IT WAS:

Do you remember venders selling Givellawater [bleach] in the back alleys? It's probably the way Clorox got started.

Italian Style Lamb Stew with Tomatoes, Celery and Peppers

ITALIAN STYLE LAMB STEW WITH TOMATOES, CELERY, PEPPERS:

Ingredients:

Lamb chops, for this recipe we will use the tiny rib chops. They are quite expensive but are worth it. However if your budget is a little tight you may use any of the other lamb chops that may be available. If the chops are large cut them into smaller pieces. The quantity to use for this recipe depends on the size of the chops; if they are the smaller ones you can figure at least 3 per person per serving.

6 large cleaned and peeled celery stalks with their leaves, chop celery and leaves into 1-inch pieces and set aside.

3 green bell peppers remove stem and membrane then slice the peppers into 1-inch strips and set aside.

3 red bell peppers {same as above}.

6 Italian long hot peppers remove the stem and most of the seeds, cut into 3 inch pieces, let me say here that in any of my recipes that call for or include hot peppers the degree of hotness depends entirely on you. If you are like me the hotter the better but for some people it may be too hot so you be the judge on how many hot peppers to add to any recipe.

1 28 oz can of tomato sauce

1 28 oz can of crushed or chefs cut tomatoes

Salt and pepper to taste

Garlic powder the size of nickel

Oregano dried the size of dime

Parsley dried the size of a nickel

Sweet basil dried the size of a nickel

One half of one medium size onion chopped into 1/2 inch pieces

Olive oil

Cooking Lamb Stew with Tomatoes, Celery and Peppers:

In a large heavy pot or Dutch oven add just enough olive oil to thinly cover the bottom of the pot. Allow the oil to get hot then set heat to medium. Place the lamb chops into the pot allowing them to brown on both sides, add salt and pepper as desired. When this is done remove the chops from the pot and set them aside.

With heat set to medium, add the celery and onion to the pot and sauté until the onions become soft. Add both cans of tomatoes and all of the other ingredients. Cook for 30 minutes over medium heat stirring occasionally. Add in the chops and allow to simmer for at least another 30 minutes or until the chops are fully cooked and tender.

Serve with white rice, a leafy green salad and sliced crispy Italian bread.

THE WAY IT WAS:

I remember so clearly the hot summer days in the city. To cool off a little we opened the fire hydrant and played under the gushing water until the police came and shut the fire hydrant off. No one had a pool in those days, hey it was life in the big city, where would you install the pool anyway? The only pool in our area was city operated. It was always very crowded and in order to get into the pool some days you had to bring a bar of soap. We called the city pool the swimmies. My older brothers went swimming in the Delaware River, off of a pier. Could you imagine doing that now?

"Brother Frankie"

THE WAY IT WAS:

On hot summer nights, as kids growing up, we gathered at a local candy store, trying our best to cool off by slurping Italian water ice, or drinking bottles of Coke or Pepsi Cola.

There were three age groups of guys that used that corner store, "Pops" as a regular gathering or meeting place, so there were a lot of different personalities. Some of them played poker in the backroom of the store. Others played pinochle. Some guys would be in little groups talking or arguing about sports or who was the best at boxing or whatever.

And there were the pinball machine players, a couple of guys would cheat the machine by resting the two front legs of the machine on the tip of their shoes to keep the metal ball from going down the shoot so that they could get free games.

They really took a chance doing that because if they were to get caught by "Mom", the storekeepers wife, she would bop you on the head with her cane. I don't think "Mom" really needed the cane to help her walk; she just used it for protection and to keep order. She was a tough old lady but we all loved her.

Then there were three or four guys that loved to sing and harmonize, "they were rough and ready guys but oh how they could harmonize"; do you remember that line of the song "Heart of My Heart"? They would imitate the popular recording groups of the time, like the Four Aces. I could imagine seeing and hearing them singing now, do you remember the song "Tell Me Why" by the Four Aces? Wow! what a great song; after all these years I could still remember most of the words. It was a time, in my opinion, that some of the best music was ever written.

Italian Style Chicken Cacciatore (Bianca)

ITALIAN STYLE CHICKEN CACCIATORE BIANCO WITHOUT TOMATOES:

Ingredients:

Cut up chicken parts and pieces (your choice) 2 legs, 2 thighs, 2 breasts cut into 4 pieces, 2 wings or one chicken cut into 10 pieces.

For the recipe below we will use 10 pieces of chicken. Rinse chicken parts in cold water and pat dry

Olive oil

1 red bell pepper sliced into strips

1 green bell pepper sliced into strips

6 hot cherry peppers in vinegar

Approximately 2 oz of liquid from the jar of the hot cherry peppers

Salt and pepper

Garlic powder

Dried oregano leaves

Bay leaves 4-5

Fresh flat leaf Italian parsley if available - if it is not use dried parsley

1 - 14 oz can of chicken or beef broth

Cooking Chicken and Peppers Cacciatore Bianca:

Add enough olive oil to lightly cover the bottom of a large pot, allow the oil to get hot over medium heat. Gently place all of the chicken parts into the hot olive oil, be careful of splashing the hot oil. Very lightly brown all of the chicken parts.

If necessary, (because your pot may not be large enough) just brown a few pieces of chicken at a time. Season the chicken parts lightly with the garlic powder, salt and pepper. Remove the slightly browned seasoned chicken parts from the pan and set aside. Add the red and green pepper strips to the hot olive oil and sauté until the pepper strips get tender or soften, add salt to the peppers if desired.

Return the chicken parts to the pot - shake a little of the dried oregano and parsley leaves onto the chicken - add all of the remaining ingredients - reduce the heat to simmer.

Allow the chicken to simmer until it is thoroughly cooked and the meat is about to fall off of the bone, approximately 30 minutes or more.

Serve on a bed of white rice and a side of sweet green peas and a mixed green salad.

TIDBITS:

A variation of chicken cacciatore can also be made with tomatoes. I guess it can still be called cacciatore.

Italian Style Chicken Cacciatore with Tomatoes (Russo)

ITALIAN STYLE CHICKEN CACCIATORE RUSSO WITH TOMATOES:

The big difference between the red and white chicken cacciatore is simply omitting the hot cherry peppers and vinegar from the recipe, adding in its place one 28 ounce can of crushed tomatoes, and to make it tangy you can include fresh long hot green Italian peppers. The chicken cacciatore without the vinegar peppers will of course have a different flavor but will be equally delicious.

Italian Style Chicken Cutlets

ITALIAN STYLE CHICKEN CUTLETS:

(Christie's Favorite)

Ingredients:

Chicken breasts sliced thin from your butcher or supermarket. Depending on the size of the chicken breast you can estimate at least 2 cutlets per person.

For this recipe we will use 12 chicken cutlets.

Bread crumbs, I prefer to use unflavored breadcrumbs without cheese.

Garlic powder

Fresh Italian flat leaf parsley finely chopped about the size of a silver dollar- fresh parsley is really great when used in this recipe - if not available, you can use the dried leaf parsley about the size of a quarter

Dried leaf oregano about the size of a dime

Salt and pepper as needed

Grated Locatelli Romano cheese

Grated or crushed hot red pepper flakes (optional)

Olive oil for frying, corn oil can be used as a substitute

Preparing Chicken Cutlets:

For this recipe you will need two bowls. One to hold the dry mix and flavored breadcrumbs and one for the beaten egg mixture. As in all of my recipes all amounts are just approximations. You could use more or less depending on your taste. Mix enough breadcrumbs about 6 or 8 oz's with about 3 or 4 oz's of the Locatelli Romano cheese.

Add and mix in the fresh parsley and the oregano

Add and mix in the garlic powder to taste

Add and mix in the crushed red hot pepper to taste (optional)

Add and mix in the salt and pepper to taste, keep in mind that Romano cheese is a little salty - mix it altogether in the aluminum pan and set aside momentarily.

In a frying pan add enough olive oil to cover the bottom of the pan. You do not need a lot of oil. Get the oil hot over a medium heat and while the oil is getting hot, in a suitable bowl, mix 2 large eggs and a little milk, about one ounce will do for dipping the chicken. Dip in one chicken cutlet at a time and cover with the egg mixture thoroughly. Shake off any extra egg mixture. Dredge the egg covered chicken cutlet in the breadcrumb mixture covering the cutlet thoroughly.

Place the cutlet into the pan with the hot oil and let it brown on one side before turning it over to brown the other side. Remove from pan when both sides are browned. Repeat this procedure until all the cutlets are fried.

Do not try to fry too many cutlets at any one time, depending on the size of the pan 2 or 3 cutlets at a time is about right.

It would be a great idea to place the fried cutlets on a couple of paper towels or a rack to absorb or drain any excess oil. Serve the cutlets with a side of steamed green beans.

Also a great idea for a side dish and always a favorite with any meal would be a combination of stewed hot and sweet peppers and tomatoes. The recipe is found elsewhere in this cookbook.

THE WAY IT WAS:

Do you remember when you could walk around in the city without worrying about getting mugged or shot? And did we walk; it was one of our favorite things to do. Sometimes we would walk from one end of the city to the other. Everyone knew all the street names in order. The streets seemed to be much safer then they are now. Why do you think that is?

Italian Style Eggplant Parmigiana

ITALIAN STYLE EGGPLANT PARMIGIANA:

(Lisa's Favorite)

Ingredients:

2 medium sized eggplants peeled and sliced horizontally in ¼ inch pieces

8 oz of grated Mozzarella cheese

8 oz of grated Locatelli Romano cheese

2 eggs beaten with a little milk salt and pepper

8 oz of plain breadcrumbs enough to coat the sliced eggplants, or you can use seasoned bread crumbs if you prefer

Corn oil for frying

Dried oregano

Dried parsley

One 28 oz can of tomato sauce

Cooking Eggplant Parmigiana:

Add enough oil to a frying pan to fry the eggplants, although the recipe calls for corn oil you can use any oil that you prefer. Get the oil hot and ready for frying.

Dip the sliced eggplant into the beaten egg mixture shake off any extra.

Dredge the egg covered eggplant slices through the seasoned breadcrumbs. If you are not using seasoned breadcrumbs you will need to season the plain breadcrumbs, add to the plain breadcrumbs about the size of a quarter of the dried parsley and about the size of a dime of the dried oregano, measured in the palm of your hand.

Shake off any extra breadcrumbs, fry the eggplant slices until they are a golden brown. As they become fried set them aside on paper towels to absorb or to drain oil. Continue until all the eggplant slices are fried.

Prepare a large enough baking pan (Lasagna pans will do just fine). Spoon in from the can of tomato sauce enough sauce to lightly coat the bottom of the pan.

Layer in one layer of fried eggplant, then spoon tomato sauce lightly over the eggplant, then sprinkle lightly with the grated Locatelli Romano cheese, then very lightly sprinkle the grated mozzarella cheese, repeat the process until all of the eggplant has been placed into the baking pan.

At the very top of the layers add a little extra tomato sauce and mozzarella grated cheese, cover lightly with aluminum foil and poke a few holes into the cover to let out steam. Set the oven temperature at 325 degrees and let it bake for about 30 minutes or until the top layer of mozzarella cheese is melted and the tomato sauce is bubbly.

THE WAY IT WAS:

Do you remember the name Lamont Cranston and sitting on the floor in front of the radio listening to the Shadow? Ha! Ha! Ha! only the Shadow knows. His laugh was kind of scary.

Italian Style Zucchini with Tomatoes and Eggs

ITALIAN STYLE ZUCCHINI, TOMATOES AND EGGS:

Ingredients:

Olive oil

6 - peeled medium sized green squash or zucchini cut horizontally into ¼ inch slices. Some or all of the skin may be left on the zucchini if you desire.

1 - 28 oz. can of Italian tomatoes

2 - large eggs lightly beaten

Salt and pepper to taste

½ of a medium size red bell pepper chopped into small ½ inch pieces

1 or 2 Italian green long hot peppers [optional] chopped into small ½ inch pieces

Garlic powder

Dried oregano

Grated Locatelli Romano cheese

Cooking Zucchini, Tomatoes and Eggs:

In a large sauté pot over medium heat add enough olive oil to just cover the bottom of the sauté pot, a bit more or less is okay. Add the sliced zucchini and stir.

Add the red bell peppers and stir

Add the hot green peppers and stir (optional)

Add salt and pepper to taste

Add the can of Italian tomatoes

Sprinkle lightly with garlic powder

Add the oregano about the size of a dime measured in the palm of hand

Stirring occasionally

Cook until the zucchini becomes tender

Add the lightly beaten eggs

Add or sprinkle with the Locatelli Romano cheese - Cook for additional minute or until the eggs are cooked.

Serve as side vegetable or a one dish meal.

THE WAY IT WAS:

Do you remember the number writers or so called bookies that walked up and down the street collecting nickel and dime bets, people yelling out their favorite dream number? I never did see him write anything down; I still wonder, how did he remember all those numbers?

Italian Style Green Beans with Potatoes and Tomato Gravy

ITALIAN STYLE GREEN BEANS AND POTATOES IN TOMATO GRAVY:

Ingredients:

About three pounds of peeled regular white potatoes cut into ¼ inch

1½ pounds of fresh green beans with the tips cut off clean and rinse

Olive oil

1-28 oz can of tomato sauce

Dried oregano about the size of a dime

Dried parsley about the size of a nickel

Garlic powder to sprinkle

Salt and pepper to taste

Cooking Green Beans and Potatoes in Tomato Gravy:

In a large pot add enough olive oil to lightly cover the bottom of the pot. Using medium heat add the can of tomato sauce to the hot oil.

Season with the dried oregano, parsley, garlic powder. Lower the heat and let simmer stirring occasionally.

In another pot add water, salt and potatoes. Parboil the potatoes until they are halfway done. Drain in colander and set aside temporarily. Add string beans to salted boiling water and parboil until tender. Add the potatoes and the string beans to the tomato sauce. Add salt and pepper to taste. Let it simmer until potatoes and string beans are fully cooked.

Serve as a side dish with a steak or fried chicken or as a one-dish meal.

TIDBITS:

Did you know that some foods burn more calories than they contain? Celery is one of them. A list of others can be found elsewhere in this book.

Italian Style Peas and Artichokes

ITALIAN STYLE PEAS AND ARTICHOKES:

(A Gilda Rose Favorite)

Ingredients:

2 packages of frozen artichoke hearts

2 packages of frozen peas

Olive oil

Garlic powder

Salt and Pepper

Cooking Peas and Artichokes:

Defrost artichokes and peas

In a large skillet add olive oil to lightly cover the bottom of the pot

Heat over medium heat until the oil is hot

Place the artichokes and peas into the pot and cook until tender

Shake garlic powder to taste - stir, add salt and pepper to taste - stir

Cover and test occasionally until desired doneness.

Italian Style Fried Cauliflower

ITALIAN STYLE FRIED CAULIFLOWER:

(Gina's Favorite)

Ingredients:

Olive oil, or corn oil or any favorite oil for frying

Large head of cauliflower cleaned and broken into florets

Salt and pepper to taste

2 eggs beaten with a little milk and a little salt and pepper

Breadcrumbs seasoned with salt and pepper, finely chopped parsley, garlic powder and (grated Locatelli Romano cheese optional) or seasoned flour.

Frying Cauliflower:

There are a few options here: You can use all olive oil to fry but you must be careful, olive oil tends to smoke if the pan gets too hot. Keep the heat at medium and you probably won't have any trouble or you can use just corn oil and not worry too much about the oil smoking. Or you can use a combination of olive oil and corn oil to fry as I have done on many occasions; that combination saves some expense on the cost of using all olive oil. In a large frying pan add enough of your favorite oil to fry the cauliflower. Using medium heat, allow the oil to get hot.

In preparing most items for frying, sometimes the item going to be fried is first dipped in flour then in egg mixture then in breadcrumbs. I believe the reason for flour is to protect the item from getting saturated with oil. The routine as stated above can be changed many ways. It depends on what you want to achieve as a desired end result.

Experiment with it a couple of ways until you find what's best for the item you are frying. As an example of what I am trying to convey is; you can dip the cauliflower into the egg mixture then into breadcrumbs without using flour, or you could use the egg and flour and not use the breadcrumbs, or you could use flour, egg, then breadcrumbs. Capish, si or no?

TIDBITS:

You may want to use a large plastic freezer storage bag to help with coating the pieces of cauliflower. Place the seasoned flour into the bag. Add several pieces of cauliflower at a time - shake the bag until each piece is coated with flour. Be sure to shake off any extra flour before dipping in the egg mixture. Dip the flour-coated cauliflower into the beaten egg mixture shake off any extra egg mixture, now dredge the cauliflower through the breadcrumbs. Place the breaded cauliflower into the heated oil and fry to a golden brown turning once so as to be sure both sides get that golden brown color.

Serve as an added vegetable treat with any main course or serve as a wonderful hot hors d'oeuvres.

THE WAY IT WAS:

Remember when all Christmas trees were real and sold for a dollar or less on Christmas Eve? Some trees were so scrawny we often had to tie two together to make it look like one good one.

Italian Style Celery and Lima Beans with Tomatoes

ITALIAN STYLE CELERY AND LIMA BEANS WITH TOMATOES:

Ingredients:

½ medium size onion, sliced into strips

1 stalk of celery with leaves, cleaned, washed under cold water and cut into bite size pieces

2 -10 or 12 oz. packages of frozen lima beans, regular or baby limas

1- 28 oz. can of crushed tomatoes

1 - 8 oz. can of tomato sauce

Salt and pepper to taste

Garlic powder optional and to taste

Crushed red hot pepper also optional

Dried parsley about the size of a nickel

Oregano about the size of a dime

Olive oil

Cooking Celery and Lima Beans with Tomatoes:

In a pot or pan large enough to accommodate all of the above ingredients, using medium heat, coat the bottom of the pan with enough olive oil to sauté the celery and onions. When the onions and celery become tender or soften add the can of crushed tomatoes.

Add the small can of tomato sauce

Add all of the lima beans

Add salt and pepper to taste

Add all of the remaining herbs and spices

Cover the pot and lower the heat to simmer

Let cook until lima beans are softened or desired tenderness.

Italian Style Fried Peppers and Eggs

ITALIAN STYLE FRIED PEPPERS AND EGGS:

Ingredients:

2 medium sweet red bell peppers cut into small ½ inch pieces

1 medium sweet green bell pepper cut into small ½ inch pieces

1 green Italian long hot pepper cut into very small ¼ inch pieces (optional)

6 large eggs beaten

Salt and pepper

Olive oil for frying

Frying Peppers and Eggs:

In a frying pan over medium heat add enough olive oil to just coat the bottom of the pan and allow it to get hot - add in all of the cut pieces of peppers. Allow the peppers to fry and get to where you like them best; I like them well done almost burnt but not quite burned.

Add the beaten eggs

Add salt and pepper to taste

Serve on a crispy Italian roll. A nice fresh tomato and sweet basil salad would be great to serve as well.

TIDBITS:

Without any doubt this is my favorite sandwich filler and soon to be yours; give it a try soon. Italian ham [prosciutto], salami, capicola and provolone are all great and make wonderful sandwiches, but when you bite into a pepper and egg sandwich, something magical happens to your palate mmmm, you will then agree there is nothing that you can make a sandwich with that is better tasting than peppers and eggs.

Italian Style Fried Potatoes and Eggs

ITALIAN STYLE FRIED POTATOES AND EGGS:

Ingredients:

6 medium-sized potatoes peeled, rinsed and then sliced thin

3 large eggs

Olive or corn oil for frying

Salt and pepper - Grated or crushed hot red pepper flakes (optional)

Frying Potatoes and Eggs:

In a large frying pan or skillet over medium heat add enough oil to coat the pan for frying the potatoes. When the oil is hot enough add the potatoes and fry 'til golden brown. Add more oil if needed - do not drench the potatoes in the oil.

Add just a little salt and pepper as desired.

When the potatoes are done as you like them bring the heat to low.

In a mixing bowl add the 3 large eggs - beat the eggs to a smooth consistency then pour the egg mixture onto the fried potatoes, stir the mixture of eggs and potatoes, add more salt if needed and the red pepper flakes if desired - Fry until egg mixture is thoroughly cooked - Serve with a salad or as a sandwich filler.

Italian Style Fried Tomatoes and Eggs

ITALIAN STYLE FRIED EGGS AND TOMATO SAUCE:

Ingredients:

1 - 8 oz can tomato sauce

4 to 6 large eggs

1/4 small onion - sliced

Olive oil

Salt and pepper to taste

Preparing:

In a frying pan over medium heat sauté onion in olive oil.

Add one can of tomato sauce until thoroughly heated.

In a mixing bowl, beat the eggs adding the salt and pepper.

Add the beaten eggs slowly to the tomato sauce, stirring constantly until the eggs are thoroughly absorbed into the tomato sauce.

Other ingredients such as red pepper flakes, parsley, chives can all be added to taste. Serve as a sandwich filler.

Italian Style Fried Eggs and Grated Romano Cheese

ITALIAN STYLE FRIED EGGS AND GRATED ROMANO CHEESE:

(Original cheese frittata)

Ingredients:

4 to 6 large eggs

Olive oil

Salt and pepper

4 ounces grated Romano cheese or Parmesan

Red pepper flakes (optional)

Preparing:

In a frying pan over medium heat use a small amount of olive oil, just enough to fry four or six large eggs. In a mixing bowl beat the eggs adding the cheese.

Add salt and pepper to taste (be careful when adding salt as the cheese is salty).

Add the optional red pepper flakes.

Fry until golden brown.

Italian Style Fried Eggs, Onions and Mushrooms

ITALIAN STYLE FRIED EGGS WITH ONIONS AND MUSHROOMS:

Ingredients:

6 large eggs beaten

10 ounce pkg. fresh button mushrooms sliced thin

1 small onion sliced thin

Olive oil

Salt and pepper to taste

Preparing:

In frying pan over medium heat add small amount of olive oil enough to fry the mushrooms to a golden brown - then add onions - stir and fry for about 5 minutes.

Add in beaten eggs - add salt and pepper to taste - cook until done.

Italian Style Fried Eggs and Fillets of Anchovies

ITALIAN STYLE FRIED EGGS AND FILLETS OF ANCHOVIES:

Ingredients:

6 large eggs beaten

1 can of fillet of anchovies packed in olive oil

Crushed red pepper flakes (optional)

Olive oil

Preparing:

In a frying pan over medium heat, add a very small amount of olive oil - add can of anchovies - cook until anchovies melt - then add eggs and optional red pepper flakes.

Italian Style Lupini Bean Salad

ITALIAN STYLE LUPINI BEANS SALAD OR APPETIZER:

TIDBITS:

Lupini beans get their name from the Italian word Lupe which means wolf. The lupini bean is in the pea family, round and shaped like the eye of a wolf. A jar of lupini beans can be found in supermarkets generally in the olive section or Italian foods section. Most Italian deli's carry this item.

Ingredients:

A jar of lupini beans (jars come in a couple of sizes)

Olive oil

Salt and pepper

Hot red pepper flakes (optional)

Garlic powder

Fresh flat leaf Italian parsley finely chopped about the size of a quarter

Oregano about the size of a dime

Preparing:

Place the contents of the jar of lupini beans in a colander. Rinse thoroughly with cold water - Place the drained lupini beans into a serving bowl.

Sprinkle with olive oil, add salt and pepper to taste. Add the finely chopped parsley and oregano.

Add the garlic powder and red pepper flakes as desired.

Serve as an appetizer or a healthy snack.

Italian Style Ceci or Chick Pea Salad or Appetizer

ITALIAN STYLE CHICK PEAS (CECI) SALAD OR APPETIZER:

Ingredients:

One or two cans of chickpeas

One can of pitted ripe black olives

Olive oil

Salt and pepper

Hot red pepper flakes (optional)

Garlic powder

Fresh flat leaf Italian parsley finely chopped about the size of a quarter

Preparing:

Place the contents of the opened can of chickpeas into a colander - rinse thoroughly under cold water - drain well then place the chickpeas into a serving bowl. Sprinkle with olive oil.

Add salt and pepper to taste - Add the finely chopped parsley.

Add the garlic powder and red pepper flakes as desired.

Serve as an appetizer or a delicious snack.

Italian Style Potato Salad

ITALIAN STYLE POTATO SALAD:

Try making this easy recipe just once and you will be making it all the time - delicious, economical and certainly will be enjoyed by everyone.

Ingredients:

Three pounds more or less of regular white potatoes, peeled, washed and rinsed under cold water, cut into bite size pieces

3 or 4 whole garlic cloves, sliced into very thin slices so when fried they become crisp

¼ of a medium size onion, chopped into ½ inch pieces (optional)

Salt and pepper to taste

Garlic powder

Fresh flat leaf Italian parsley, dried parsley will do if fresh is not available

Crushed red hot pepper flakes (optional)

Olive oil for frying

Cooking and Preparing Italian Potato Salad:

Cook potatoes in a large pot of salted boiling water. Drain and set aside.

Before the potatoes are completely cooked prepare the other ingredients. In a small frying pan over medium heat place enough olive oil about 2 or 3 oz (this amount is always determined by the amount of potatoes that were cooked to begin with) adjusting the amount of oil accordingly.

When the oil is hot enough, add the garlic to the hot oil and fry until golden brown being careful not to burn the thin cut garlic - at this point you can add the optional onions and fry them along with the garlic.

Add if desired, a bit of garlic powder. Add the crushed red hot pepper flakes.

The garlic cloves and the onions must be fried completely before adding the crushed red pepper flakes; because the pepper flakes will cook almost instantly and burn if left in the hot oil too long.

After the potatoes have drained completely place them in a serving platter and right from the pan cover the potatoes with the hot olive oil mixture.

Add salt and black pepper to taste. Add the dried parsley to the mixture or top the potatoes off with a garnish of chopped fresh parsley.

Serve this potato salad anytime, it's sure to please!

THE WAY IT WAS:

Quite often Mom made her own pasta, all by hand. She would mix a large pile of flour with eggs and water into a large dough ball, let it sit for a while covered with a dish cloth then kneaded and rolled it out into several long rope like lengths.

Then she cut the rope into small 1 inch pieces and with her magic thumb shaped the small pieces into little hat like pasta. In those days we had a very large porcelain topped kitchen table. The little pasta hats sat in rows filling the entire top of the table until they were dried enough to cook.

If there was any dough left over Mom would shape the dough into small pizzas and fry them in olive oil topped with salt and hot red crushed pepper. Sometimes, Mom would use the dough to make doughnuts by dipping them in powdered sugar. It was a great treat to get a small piece of the fried dough. And the homemade pasta had a taste that was out of this world.

Italian Style Eggplant and Celery with Tomatoes

ITALIAN STYLE EGGPLANT, CELERY, OLIVES IN TOMATO SAUCE:

(Mary's Favorite)

Ingredients:

1 medium or large size eggplant cubed or cut into bite size pieces

3 or 4 stalks of washed celery with leaves, cut into bite size pieces

1 medium size onion diced

1 red or green bell pepper cut into small bite size pieces

1 - 28 oz. can of tomato sauce

1 can pitted black ripe olives cut into halves

Salt and pepper to taste

2 or 3 dried bay leaves

6 fresh sweet basil leaves chopped or dry if not available

Crushed hot red pepper (optional)

Cooking Eggplant, Celery, Olives in Tomato Sauce:

In a sauce pan cover bottom of sauce pan with olive oil. Over medium heat sauté the eggplant, onion, bell pepper and celery until tender.

Add tomato sauce - Add salt and pepper to taste - Add the bay leaves - Add the sweet basil - Add the optional hot red pepper flakes - Add the olives

Lower heat to simmer. Place the lid on the sauce pan and let it simmer until desired doneness. Serve as main dish or a great side to any meal.

Italian Style Lentil Soup

ITALIAN STYLE LENTIL SOUP:

(Cassie's Favorite)

Ingredients:

1 package of dried lentils - Place the lentils on tabletop and check for tiny pebbles, stones or other foreign materials then place in colander and rinse under cold water.

1 red or green bell pepper chopped into fine pieces

1 or 2 washed and peeled carrots, chopped into very small bite size pieces

1 or 2 celery stalks, washed and chopped into very small pieces

1 small onion chopped into fine pieces

1 bouillon cube beef or chicken

1 - 8oz can tomato sauce

2 or 3 bay leaves

Salt and pepper to taste

Preparing and Cooking Lentil Soup:

In a soup pot lightly cover the bottom of the pot with olive oil.

Over medium heat:

Add the celery - Add the bell pepper - Add the onion - Add the carrots

Sauté vegetables until tender or soft

Add 4 quarts of water

Add the lentils

Add bay leaves

Add the bouillon cube

Add the tomato sauce

Salt and pepper to taste

Lower heat and simmer until lentils are tender (about two hours).

Lentil soup may be served as is or for added goodness you can add any small shaped pasta or rice. Small shaped pasta could be Ditalini, elbows or small shells or even Spaghetti broken into small pieces.

Italian Style Holiday Olive Salad or Antipasto

ITALIAN STYLE HOLIDAY OLIVE SALAD (Antipasto Salad):

Ingredients:

Black ripe olives cut into halves or quarters

Green olives with pimento cut into halves or quarters

Artichoke hearts cut into halves

Celery chopped into very small pieces

Roasted red peppers sliced into small pieces

Hot cherry peppers (stems and seeds removed) chopped into small pieces

Capers rinsed under cold water drained and leave whole

Carrots cut into very small pieces

Olive oil

Crushed black pepper

Marinated mushrooms - optional

Hearts of palm - optional

Garlic powder - optional

Anchovies - optional chopped finely or just use the oil

Mozzarella - optional - cut into small bite size pieces

Preparing:

In a large serving bowl add all of the above ingredients - mix well.

Sprinkle or drizzle lightly with olive oil.

TIDBITS:

I purposely left out the quantities for the ingredients above because they can be used in any quantity according to individual tastes. The secret is in the combination of all the ingredients. Try it, you will love it.

Italian Style Potatoes Pizziole

ITALIAN STYLE POTATOES PIZZIOLE:

(Marianne's Favorite)

Ingredients:

3 - pounds of regular white potatoes washed peeled and cut into slices

1 - 16 oz can of Italian tomato sauce

Grated Mozzarella cheese 8oz

Grated Romano or Parmesan cheese about 2 oz

Parsley fresh flat leaf Italian if available or dried grated will do. If fresh is used, chop a small amount to sprinkle on top of potatoes, if using dried use about the size of a dime

Oregano about the size of a dime

Salt and pepper to taste

Olive oil to lightly cover the bottom of a roasting pan

Cooking Potatoes Pizziole:

Set oven temperature to medium about 325 degrees. Place the cut potatoes in the roasting pan and cover. Let potatoes roast for about 30 minutes, or until almost cooked.

Uncover the pan and stir the potatoes - leave cover off. Allow the potatoes to brown sufficiently. After the potatoes have browned, remove temporarily from oven. Ladle spoonfuls of tomato sauce over top of potatoes.

Add salt and pepper to taste - Add the Mozzarella cheese

Add Romano or the Parmesan cheese - Add the oregano

Return to oven until tomato sauce and cheese start to bubble, (about 30 minutes). Serve as a side with any meat, fish or fowl.

Italian Style Swiss-Chard and Beans

ITALIAN STYLE SWISS CHARD AND CANNELLINI BEANS

Ingredients:

1 or 2 bunches of Swiss chard washed and cut into bite size pieces

1 can of cannellini beans rinsed under cold water and drain in colander

Olive oil

Garlic powder or 3 or 4 cloves of fresh garlic cut into ¼ inch pieces

Salt and pepper to taste

Red hot pepper flakes to taste - (optional)

Preparing and Cooking Swiss Chard and Beans:

In a large pot over medium heat add the Swiss chard and enough water to steam the leaves - add salt - lower heat to simmer.

Over low heat lightly cover the bottom of a frying pan with olive oil - add the garlic cloves or garlic powder and lightly brown the garlic, careful not to burn.

Add the can of cannellini beans to the garlic and sauté for a few minutes.

Add the optional hot red pepper flakes.

Add the mixture of sautéed beans, garlic, red pepper and olive oil to the steamed Swiss chard - mix and serve.

TIDBITS:

Always be careful when adding washed vegetables to hot oil; they may have been draining but will always retain a little water.

The Way It Was:

When I was growing up, my Mom often cooked or used in salads all kinds of green vegetables including cabbage, dandelion, escarole, Swiss chard, spinach, broccoli rabe, etc. I remember so clearly how I tried to avoid eating them and how much I hated them. How dumb was I?

Italian Style Tripe

ITALIAN STYLE TRIPE:

This is truly considered to be peasant food. When prepared properly, it is delicious. In case you are wondering, it is the stomach lining of a cow or steer.

Ingredients:

2 pounds of honeycomb tripe, fat trimmed off washed thoroughly in cold water. Tripe when purchased should be white in color.

After washing allow the tripe to soak in cold salted water for at least 30 minutes. Rinse again and drain completely. Pat and dry the tripe.

1 - 28 oz can of tomato sauce

2 - or three red bell peppers sliced into 1 inch slices

6 - long hot green Italian peppers - slice into bite size pieces

4 - stalks of fresh celery with leaves washed and cut into bite sized pieces

Olive oil

Salt and pepper to taste

Garlic powder to taste

Dried oregano about the size of a dime

6 fresh sweet basil leaves cut into fine pieces

Preparing and Cooking Tripe:

Slice tripe into ½ inch strips 2 or 3 inches long. In a large pot over medium heat coat the bottom of the pot with olive oil. Add the sliced tripe. Cook tripe for 30 minutes.

Add salt and ground black pepper

Add the garlic powder

Add red bell peppers

Add green hot peppers

Add cut celery

Add can of tomato sauce

Add the oregano

Add the sweet basil

Bring to a boil stirring the pot as often as needed. After it has come to a boil lower heat to simmer with lid on. Allow tripe to cook until tender.

TIDBITS:

The secret to making delicious tripe is not to rush it. Allow all the flavors to blend together. Allow it to cook until it almost melts in your mouth.

Sometimes when fresh peppers cook too long the skins will peel off and curl; it's no big thing if this should happen simply remove the skins.

The added hot peppers will make this recipe very hot or tangy and that's great if you like it hot. But if you prefer it less tangy, then just replace the hot peppers with sweet green bell peppers.

Most everyone ate tripe sandwiches from the local bar. It was always a treat especially when the bread was a crispy Italian roll and the beer was ice cold.

Italian Style Calamari with Potatoes and Peas

ITALIAN STYLE CALAMARI WITH POTATOES AND PEAS:

(Bobby D's Favorite)

Ingredients:

2 - pounds of cleaned calamari - cut into rings with tentacles cut into pieces

3 - pounds of white regular potatoes washed peeled and cut into quarters

1 - 16 oz can of sweet peas drained

1 - 28 oz can of Italian style crushed tomatoes

Olive oil

Salt and pepper

Garlic powder or 3 or 4 fresh garlic cloves cut into ¼ inch pieces

1 green bell pepper sliced into 1 inch pieces

1 red bell pepper sliced into 1 inch pieces

1 stalk of celery cut into bite size pieces

Crushed red hot pepper flakes to taste - (optional)

Fresh sweet basil - 6 leaves cut into fine pieces - use the dried basil if fresh is not available - use about the size of a nickel

Dried oregano about the size of a dime

Preparing and Cooking:

In a large pot add enough water and salt to boil the potatoes.

Partially boil potatoes, drain in colander and set aside.

In a large pot, add enough olive oil and sauté the calamari. (You may use the same pot that you boiled the potatoes in, just rinse and dry).

Add the green bell pepper

Add the red bell pepper

Add the celery

Add the garlic

Sauté for 15 minutes

Add the crushed tomatoes

Add the sweet basil

Add the oregano

Add the optional red pepper flakes

Add salt and pepper to taste, remembering that the potatoes had salt added to them when they were boiling. Bring the ingredients above to a slow boil - lower the heat and simmer until the calamari rings are tender. When the calamari has cooked to your desired consistency add the potatoes. Let the potatoes simmer until they are completely cooked then add the peas and cook for an additional 10 minutes.

Serve as first course with a green salad and crisp Italian bread.

TIDBITS:

Calamari can be a little tricky to get it just right. Sometimes if not cooked long enough it becomes chewy. But if you cook it quickly it can be tender. What I am saying is that if you are going to use calamari in a stew as the recipe above is, then the calamari will have to cook longer to become tender. But if you were going to fry calamari, then it would have to be cooked or fried quickly, otherwise it will become chewy. I guess there is no in-between, either cook it fast or cook it slow. Either way it's going to be delicious.

THE WAY IT WAS:

I am one of nine brothers and two sisters so you will agree that I came from a pretty large sized family. Very often, just when we all sat down to eat dinner, it seems we never had enough bread to go around, and so I was always the one chosen to go to the Italian bakery to buy a nickel or ten cent loaf of Italian bread. I could not understand why I was always chosen to go and buy the bread and not one of my other brothers.

Oh well, I guess that is why today I have the compulsion to buy more bread then we really need. My wife thinks it's a little strange to have so much bread in the house, but that's probably the reason why. Quite honestly having bread in the house all the time gives me a great feeling of warmth, contentment and wealth.

"Little Al"

Italian Style Stuffed Roasted Peppers

ITALIAN STYLE ROASTED STUFFED BELL PEPPERS:

Ingredients:

4 - large red or green bell peppers washed pat dry and cut in half vertically carefully remove stem, seeds and pith

8 - oz. plain bread crumbs

4 - oz. Locatelli Romano cheese

2 - large eggs

1 - 28 oz can of tomato sauce

Olive oil

Salt and pepper to taste

Crushed hot pepper - (optional)

Fresh flat leaf Italian parsley

Garlic powder

Oregano dried the size of a dime

Preparing and Cooking Stuffed Peppers:

In a large mixing bowl add all of the above ingredients except the tomato sauce and the peppers of course, mix well.

Preheat and set oven temperature to 325 degrees. In a baking pan large enough to hold the 8 halves of peppers, coat the bottom of the pan lightly with the olive oil.

Arrange the pepper halves in the pan.

Sprinkle a drop or two of olive oil onto each pepper half - coating the outside as well as the inside of the pepper.

Fill each pepper half with the bread crumb mixture.

Add a spoonful of tomato sauce to the top of each pepper half.

Cover and place in 325 degree oven for 30 minutes.

Remove from oven and add the remainder of tomato sauce to each pepper.

Return to oven uncovered for 15 minutes or until peppers are fully roasted.

Italian Style Hot Chili

ITALIAN STYLE CHILI:

What makes this recipe Italian? I am not sure but everyone enjoys eating it.

(Gia's Favorite)

Ingredients:

1 ½ or 2 pounds of fresh ground beef, pork and veal

1 - 46 oz. can of dark red kidney beans rinsed in colander under cold water

1 - 46 oz. can of light red kidney beans rinsed in colander under cold water

1 - 46 oz. can of pork and beans

1 - 28 oz. can of tomato sauce

1 - 14 oz. can of beef broth

1 - large fresh carrot finely chopped

2 - stalks of fresh celery finely chopped

½ of Vidalia or any sweet onion finely chopped

1 - red bell pepper chopped into small pieces

1 - green bell pepper chopped into very small 1/4" pieces

6 - hot cherry peppers, stem and seeds removed finely chopped

Fresh flat leaf Italian parsley finely chopped about a dozen or so leaves

Chili powder - about the size of a quarter in the palm of your hand

Ketchup about 2 oz.

Hot sauce about 2 oz.

Steak sauce about 2 oz.

Worchester sauce 1 oz.

Salt and pepper to taste.

Preparing and Cooking Chili Italian Style:

In a very large lidded pot over medium heat add enough olive oil to sauté all of the ground meat - add the ground meat. When the ground meat has turned gray in color, add salt and pepper to taste. Stir occasionally.

Add the parsley

Add the onion

Add the red and green bell peppers

Add the celery

Add the carrots

Add the hot cherry peppers

Add the beef broth

Add the chili powder

Add the can of tomato sauce

Add the rinsed dark and light kidney beans

Add in about 2 oz. of ketchup

Add in about 2 oz. of hot sauce

Add in about 2 oz. of A1 steak sauce

Add in about 1 oz. Worchester sauce

Bring to a slow boil, cover and let cook until kidney beans are tender. - (about one hour)

Finally when the kidney beans become tender it will be time to add the last ingredient. Add the can of pork and beans, if possible remove the little pork pieces that are in the can.

Cook another 10 minutes and serve.

TIDBITS:

Sauces such as the Tabasco hot sauce, Worchester and steak sauces are arbitrary insofar as amounts are concerned. The amounts used become a matter of personal taste. Some individuals may enjoy chili that is a little bit more tangy than others, and still others may prefer more of the steak sauce or Worchester sauce. Don't be afraid to experiment.

Italian Style Peppers and Tomatoes

ITALIAN STYLE PEPPERS AND TOMATOES:

This recipe is for a side dish that can accompany almost everything - main dishes as well as sandwiches.

Ingredients:

6 - Italian long hot peppers washed and patted dry, stems and seeds removed and cut in half

2 - green bell or sweet Italian frying peppers washed and patted dry, stems, seeds and pith removed sliced vertically into ¾ or 1 inch slices

3 - red bell peppers washed and patted dry, stems, seeds and pith removed sliced vertically into ¾ or 1 inch slices

1 - 6 oz. can of Italian tomato paste

1 - 28 oz. can of tomato sauce

Olive oil for frying the peppers, salt and pepper to taste

Garlic powder to taste

Oregano about the size of a dime in the palm of your hand

Fresh sweet basil about 6 leaves chopped finely

Preparing and Cooking Peppers and Tomatoes:

In a large pot over medium heat add enough olive oil to fry all of the peppers. Add the can of tomato paste and dissolve into the olive oil. When the tomato paste has dissolved sufficiently add: peppers, salt, garlic powder, tomato sauce, oregano and the sweet basil. Lower heat to simmer - Cover and let it simmer until peppers are cooked as desired.

Italian Style Steamed Stuffed Artichokes

STEAMED AND STUFFED ARTICHOKES:

Ingredients:

6 - medium artichokes (allow at least one for each person)

4 - large eggs

4 oz. Locatelli Romano cheese

4 oz. unflavored breadcrumbs

Olive oil

Garlic powder

Dried Italian style parsley

Salt and pepper

Red hot pepper flakes (optional)

Oregano (optional)

Preparing and Cooking:

Remove any outer leaves that may be bruised, dried out, greatly discolored, torn or down-right ugly! (Smile!) Place the artichoke horizontally and with a sharp knife cut off 1/2 inch from the top allowing you to spread the leaves without getting pinched too badly. Cut and remove about 1/4 inch from the bottom stem and discard. Cut off the remainder of the stem keeping the bottom flat so that it stays upright in the pot. Rinse the chokes in a bath of cold water, spreading the leaves to remove any debris. Place in a colander, set them aside and let them drain while you are preparing the stuffing mixture.

In a large mixing bowl whisk the eggs thoroughly

Add the parsley

Add the garlic powder

Add the salt and pepper

Add the Locatelli Romano cheese

Add the unflavored breadcrumbs

Place enough water into a pot large enough to steam the artichokes, generally about an inch of water would be enough. Salt and add a few drops of olive oil to the water.

Mix all the ingredients thoroughly until the mixture is the consistency of pudding. If it is too stiff add egg, if it is too loose add a little more breadcrumbs. Set aside. Remove the chokes from the colander and prepare to stuff. Use a dish or shallow bowl under the chokes before you start to stuff them to catch any oil or stuffing.

Sprinkle each artichoke lightly with a few drops of olive oil. Salt and pepper each choke. Spread open the center part of the choke, this is where you will put the majority of the stuffing. Using a tablespoon, stuff the artichoke. Try putting some of the stuffing around the outer leaves.

Place the stuffed chokes into the pot, cover and set heat to medium. Steam for about an hour or until tender. When the outer leaves of the artichokes can be pulled off easily, it is a good sign that the chokes are done. Serve as a side or appetizer.

Note, it's a good idea to check the water level in the pot from time to time.

Italian Style Stuffed Clams (Clams Casino)

ITALIAN STYLE STUFFED CLAMS (MY VERSION OF CLAMS CASINO):

Ingredients:

24 - medium size clams

Olive oil

Four slices of bacon

2 - tablespoons butter

1/4 - of medium size onion finely chopped

1 - large red bell pepper finely chopped

2 - celery stalks finely chopped

4 - oz. unflavored breadcrumbs

Garlic powder

Salt and pepper

Paprika

Ground cayenne pepper (optional)

Preparing and Cooking Stuffed Clams:

In a small skillet, over medium heat, cook the bacon until crisp. Crumble into one inch pieces and set aside. Wash the clams under cold water. Place clams on baking sheet. Place in a preheated 350 degree oven. After a couple of minutes the clams will open. Remove from oven and set aside to cool; after they have cooled, remove the clams from the shells preserving the clam juice in a bowl. Coarsely chop the clams. Set aside.

lightly cover the bottom of a sauté pan with olive oil, add in the butter. When the butter has melted add in the onion, red bell pepper, celery, garlic powder and salt and pepper. Sprinkle in a small amount of paprika. Sauté approximately 15 to 20 minutes or until mixture softens. Add in half of the breadcrumbs, mixing thoroughly for 5 minutes. Remove from heat, pour contents into the bowl with the clams. Now, add in the remainder of the breadcrumbs. Mixture should be moist, not dry. Using a tablespoon, fill each clam shell with a rounded mound of mix. Top each stuffed shell with a small amount of crisp bacon. Place in 350 degree oven for about 10 minutes. Serve hot and enjoy!

THE WAY IT WAS:

Those days long past are sometimes referred to as the good old days by many. Perhaps so because people then were closer to each other than they seem to be at the present time. People huddled around the radio listening to a favorite broadcast, or sharing the Sunday newspaper funnies. Homes were cold but people were warmer. Scary stories being told by the elders. Delicious aromas emanating from the kitchen. The sounds of a guitar playing a familiar tune. The echoes of conversations in broken English perhaps trying to hide the subject of their conversation.

I don't believe those days really were the good old days. Those days were tough for a lot of people and especially for Italian immigrants. They had to learn the language, find a decent job, work ten - twelve hours or more a day for peanuts just to put food on the table and pay some bills. They had to study at night to become citizens, raise a family and ignore ethnic slurs. And they never complained about it. They came to the new world because they thought things were better here than where they were, but things in those days were tough all over the world. It was a time of worldwide depression and things were pretty rough everywhere.

Their desire was to provide for their family and to live in peace and freedom and prayed that someday their children would all have it just a little bit better than they did. They felt that someday their hard work and sacrifices would pay off, having their children grow up to be Americans in a free country. That's all they ever wanted. Well, "Mom" and "Pop" your prayers were answered.

My heartfelt thanks to both of you; I know you're looking down on us and smiling. We will never forget you. Thanks Mom! Thanks Pop!

CIAO!!

One Last Parting Note:

Please remember that recipes are not scientific chemical formulas where some may think making a subtle change might be strictly forbidden. In this book or any other recipe book, recipes are only guides. So if you want to add or subtract or make whatever changes you desire, feel free to do so. The real truth boils down to the end result. It has to taste good. And so we have come to a close. My wish for you is, stay healthy, be prosperous and enjoy making some of the recipes as much as I have enjoyed bringing them to you. It was truly my pleasure.

Herb Chart

Herb Chart

I am sure you heard the line "different strokes for different folks" there are probably lots of sayings just like that and all of them having the same meaning. When it comes to food and to taste, just use what's best for you. Use whatever herbs on whatever FOODS, FISH, MEAT, OR FOWL that tastes best to you.

The following herb chart is just a guide in case you are not sure what herbs to use with the different types of meat.

Beef:

Basil, Bay leaf, Caraway, Celery, Chives, Dill, Garlic, Marjoram, Onion, Paprika, Pepper, Parsley, Rosemary, Savory, Thyme.

Veal:

Allspice, Basil, Celery, Chives, Garlic, Lovage, Marjoram, Onion, Paprika, Pepper, Parsley.

Lamb:

Basil, Celery, Chervil, Chives, Cloves, Dill, Garlic, Marjoram, Mint, Onion, Paprika, Pepper, Parsley, Rosemary, Savory, Thyme.

Pork:

Rosemary, Basil, Bay leaf, Caraway, Chives, Coriander, Garlic, Ginger, Marjoram, Mustard, Onion, Oregano, Paprika, Pepper, Parsley, Sage, Savory, Thyme.

Foods the Burn Calories

Foods That Burn Calories

The following is a list of foods that burn more calories than they contain????? That means you can eat all you want without ever worrying about your diet. The list below may or may not be complete, there may be others that can be added.

Fish:

Sea bass, Flounder

Meats:

Very lean-steak

Vegetables:

Cabbage, Asparagus, Celery, Black beans, Broccoli, Green beans, Lentils, Spinach

Sweet potatoes

Fruits:

Grapefruit, Mango, Papaya, Watermelon, Pineapple, Strawberries

About the Author

About the Author

A. J. Buonpastore, married to my lovely and beautiful wife Eleanor with three beautiful daughters, Gina, Lisa, Marianne and five gorgeous granddaughters, Christie, Gia, Nikki, Brianna, Marina and one handsome grandson, Salvatore and a great son-in-law, Anthony. I was born and raised in South Philadelphia, in a family of eleven children consisting of eight brothers, Nicholas, John, Paul, Joseph, Dominic, Frank, Rocco, Anthony and two sisters, Jemma and Margaret. Mom and Pop, Catherine and Joseph.

Growing up in the city wasn't very easy for anyone who grew up in the time of the great depression. Money was tight and jobs were few. Most often men would have to work very hard and long hours just to put bread on the table and pay their rent. That is those men that were lucky enough to even have a job. Although they were tough times we always had something to eat and a place to sleep.

We could not afford to buy a house in those days. Very few people had enough money to buy a house and so renting a house was the way it was for my family until after the Second World War. My brother Joe had made and saved enough money while he was in the armed services fighting in the South Pacific to buy a house for the family. It was a very nice house in a great neighborhood of South Philly.

I got my first real job as a kid stocking shelves and delivering groceries at the corner meat market in that neighborhood. I guess that was the beginning that sparked my interest in the food business. I learned at an early age how to cut and butcher meats. Fast forward; later on I opened my very own delicatessen and produce market.

After spending a couple of years in the service during the Korean War, I spent quite a few years working within the food business then eventually managing a very well known Philadelphia fancy food and gourmet shop. The experience I gained at the gourmet shop further increased my knowledge of cooking and of fine food in general.

When adding together all the experiences I have gained about food and cooking in general throughout the years, I believe I have gathered knowledge enough to allow me the privilege of sharing with you the family tested recipes in this book.

Photographs

CPSIA information can be obtained
at www.ICGtesting.com
Printed in the USA
BVHW011927170222
629367BV00020B/289